A SHORT HISTORY OF RUSSIA
BY
Mary Platt Parmele

A SHORT HISTORY OF RUSSIA

Published by Wallachia Publishers

New York City, NY

First published 1899

Copyright © Wallachia Publishers, 2015

All rights reserved

ABOUT WALLACHIA PUBLISHERS

Wallachia Publishers mission is to publish the world's finest European history texts. More information on our recent publications and catalog can be found on our website.

If this book seems to have departed from the proper ideal of historic narrative—if it is the history of a Power, and not of a People—it is because the Russian people have had no history yet. There has been no evolution of a Russian nation, but only of a vast governing system; and the words "Russian Empire" stand for a majestic world-power in which the mass of its people have no part. A splendidly embroidered robe of Europeanism is worn over a chaotic, undeveloped mass of semi-barbarism. The reasons for this incongruity—the natural obstacles with which Russia has had to contend; the strange ethnic problems with which it has had to deal; its triumphant entry into the family of great nations; and the circumstances leading to the disastrous conflict recently concluded, and the changed conditions resulting from it—such is the story this book has tried to tell.

M. P. P.

A SHORT HISTORY OF RUSSIA

CHAPTER I.PRIMITIVE CONDITIONS AND RACES

The topography of a country is to some extent a prophecy of its future. Had there been no Mississippi coursing for three thousand miles through the North American Continent, no Ohio and Missouri bisecting it from east to west, no great inland seas indenting and watering it, no fertile prairies stretching across its vast areas, how different would have been the history of our own land.

Russia is the strange product of strange physical conditions. Nature was not in impetuous mood when she created this greater half of Europe, nor was she generous, except in the matter of space. She was slow, sluggish, but inexorable. No volcanic energies threw up rocky ridges and ramparts in Titanic rage, and then repentantly clothed them with lovely verdure as in Spain, Italy, and elsewhere. No hungry sea rushed in and tore her coast into fragments. It would seem to have been just a cold-blooded experiment in subjecting a vast region to the most rigorous and least generous conditions possible, leaving it unshielded alike from Polar winds in winter or scorching heat in summer, divesting it of beauty and of charm, and then casting this arid, frigid, torpid land to a branch of the human family as unique as its own habitation; separating it by natural and almost impassable barriers from civilizing influences, and in strange isolation leaving it to work out its own problem of development.

We have only to look on the map at the ragged coast-lines of Greece, Italy, and the British Isles to realize how powerful a factor the sea has been in great civilizations. Russia, like a thirsty giant, has for centuries been struggling to get to the tides which so generously wash the rest of Europe. During the earlier periods of her history she had not a foot of seaboard; and even now she possesses only a meager portion of coast-line for such an extent of territory; one-half of this being, except for three months in the year, sealed up with ice.

But Russia is deficient in still another essential feature. Every other European country possesses a mountain system which gives form and solidity to its structure. She alone has no such system. No skeleton or backbone gives promise of stability to the dull expanse of plains through which flow her great lazy rivers, with scarce energy enough to carry their burdens to the sea. Mountains she has, but she shares them with her neighbors; and the Carpathians, Caucasus, and Ural are simply a continuous girdle for a vast inclosure of plateaus of varying altitudes,[1] and while elsewhere it is the office of great mountain ranges to nourish, to enrich, and to beautify, in this strange land they seem designed only to imprison.

It is obvious that in a country so destitute of seaboard, its rivers must assume an immense importance. The history, the very life of Russia clusters about its three great rivers. These have been the arteries which have nourished, and indeed created, this strange empire. The Volga, with its seventy-five mouths emptying into the Caspian Sea, like a lazy leviathan brought back currents from the Orient; then the Dnieper, flowing into the Black Sea, opened up that communication with Byzantium which more than anything else has influenced the character of

Russian development; and finally, in comparatively recent times, the Neva has borne those long-sought civilizing streams from Western Europe which have made of it a modern state and joined it to the European family of nations.

It would seem that the great region we now call Russia was predestined to become one empire. No one part could exist without all the others. In the north is the zone of forests, extending from the region of Moscow and Novgorod to the Arctic Circle. At the extreme southeast, north of the Caspian Sea and at the gateway leading into Asia, are the Barren Steppes, unsuited to agriculture or to civilized living; fit only for the raising of cattle and the existence of Asiatic nomads, who to this day make it their home.

Between these two extremes lie two other zones of extraordinary character, the Black Lands and the Arable Steppes, or prairies. The former zone, which is of immense extent, is covered with a deep bed of black mold of inexhaustible fertility, which without manure produces the richest harvests, and has done so since the time of Herodotus, at which period it was the granary of Athens and of Eastern Europe.

The companion zone, running parallel with this, known as the Arable Steppes, which nearly resembles the American prairies, is almost as remarkable as the Black Lands. Its soil, although fertile, has to be renewed. But an amazing vegetation covers this great area in summer with an ocean of verdure six or eight feet high, in which men and cattle may hide as in a forest. It is these two zones in the heart of Russia that have fed millions of people for centuries, which make her now one of the greatest competitors in the markets of the world.

It is easy to see the interdependence created by this specialization in production, and the economic necessity it has imposed for an undivided empire. The forest zone could not exist without the corn of the Black Lands and the Prairies, nor without the cattle of the Steppes. Nor could those treeless regions exist without the wood of the forests. So it is obvious that when Nature girdled this eastern half of Europe, she marked it for one vast empire; and when she covered those monotonous plateaus with a black mantle of extraordinary fertility, she decreed that the Russians should be an agricultural people. And when she created natural conditions unmitigated and unparalleled in severity, she ordained that this race of toilers should be patient and submissive under austerities; that their pulse should be set to a slow, even rhythm, in harmony with the low key in which Nature spoke to them.

It is impossible to say when an Asiatic stream began to pour into Europe over the arid steppes north of the Caspian. But we know that as early as the fifth century B. C. the Greeks had established trading stations on the northern shores of the Black Sea, and that these in the fourth century had become flourishing colonies through their trade with the motley races of barbarians that swarmed about that region, who by the Greeks were indiscriminately designated by the common name of Scythians.

The Greek colonists, who always carried with them their religion, their Homer, their love of beauty, and the arts of their mother cities, established themselves on and about the promontory of the Crimea, and built their city of Chersonesos where now is Sebastopol. They first entered into wars and then alliances with these Scythians, who served them as middle-men in trade with the tribes beyond, and in time a Graeco-Scythian state of the Bosphorus came into existence.

Herodotus in the fifth century wrote much about these so-called Scythians, whom he divides into the agricultural Scythians, presumably of the Black Lands, and the nomad Scythians, of the Barren Steppes. His extravagant and fanciful pictures of those barbarians have long been studied by the curious; but light from an unexpected source has been thrown upon the subject, and Greek genius has rescued for us the type of humanity first known in Russia.

There are now in the museum at St. Petersburg two priceless works of art found in recent years in a tomb in Southern Russia. They are two vases of mingled gold and silver upon which are wrought pictures more faithful and more eloquent than those drawn by Herodotus. These figures of the Scythians, drawn probably as early as 400 B. C., reproduce unmistakably the Russian peasant of to-day. The same bearded, heavy-featured faces; the long hair coming from beneath the same peaked cap; the loose tunic bound by a girdle; the trousers tucked into the boots, and the general type, not alone distinctly Aryan, but Slavonic. And not only that; we see them breaking in and bridling their horses, in precisely the same way as the Russian peasant does to-day on those same plains. Assuredly the vexed question concerning the Scythians is in a measure answered; and we know that some of them at least were Slavonic.

But the passing illumination produced by the approach of Greek civilization did not penetrate to the region beyond, where was a tumbling, seething world of Asiatic tribes and peoples, Aryan, Tatar, and Turk, more or less mingled in varying shades of barbarism, all striving for mastery.

This elemental struggle was to resolve itself into one between Aryan and non-Aryan—the Slav and the Finn; and this again into one between the various members of the Slavonic family; then a life-and-death struggle with Asiatic barbarism in its worst form (the Mongol), with Tatar and Turk always remaining as disturbing factors.

How, and the steps by which, the least powerful branch of the Slavonic race obtained the mastery and headship of Russia and has come to be one of the leading powers of the earth, is the story this book will try to tell.

[1] In the Tatar language the word Ural signifies "girdle."

CHAPTER II.SLAVONIC RELIGIOUS AND POLITICAL SYSTEMS

In speaking of this eastern half of Europe as Russia, we have been borrowing from the future. At the time we have been considering there was no Russia. The world into which Christ came contained no Russia. The Roman Empire rose and fell, and still there was no Russia. Spain, Italy, France, and England were taking on a new form of life through the infusion of Teuton strength, and modern Europe was coming into being, and still the very name of Russia did not exist. The great expanse of plains, with its medley of Oriental barbarism, was to Europe the obscure region through which had come the Hunnish invasion from Asia.

This catastrophe was the only experience that this land had in common with the rest of Europe. The Goths had established an empire where the ancient Graeco-Scythians had once been. The overthrowing of this Gothic Empire was the beginning of Attila's European conquests; and the passage of the Hunnish horde, precisely as in the rest of Europe, produced a complete overturning. A torrent of Oriental races, Finns, Bulgarians, Magyars, and others, rushed in upon the track of the Huns, and filled up the spaces deserted by the Goths. Here as elsewhere the Hun completed his appointed task of a rearrangement of races; thus fundamentally changing the whole course of future events. Perhaps there would be no Magyar race in Hungary, and certainly a different history to write of Russia, had there been no Hunnish invasion in 375 A. D.

The old Roman Empire, which in its decay had divided into an Eastern and a Western Empire (in the fourth century), had by the fifth century succumbed to the new forces which assailed it, leaving only a glittering remnant at Byzantium.

The Eastern or Byzantine Empire, rich in pride and pretension, but poor in power, was destined to stand for one thousand years more, the shining conservator of the Christian religion (although in a form quite different from the Church of Rome) and of Greek culture. It is impossible to imagine what our civilization would be to-day if this splendid fragment of the Roman Empire had not stood in shining petrifaction during the ages of darkness, guarding the treasures of a dead past.

While these tremendous changes were occurring in the West, unconscious as toiling insects the various peoples in Russia were preparing for an unknown future. The Bulgarians were occupying large spaces in the South. The Finns, who had been driven by the Bulgarians from their home upon the Volga, had centered in the Northwest near the Baltic, their vigorous branches mingling more or less with other Asiatic races, stretching here and there in the North, South, and East. The Russian Slavs, as the parent stem is called, were distributing themselves along a strip of territory running north and south along the line of the Dnieper; while the terrible Turks, and still more terrible Tatar tribes, hovered chiefly about the Black, the Caspian, and the Sea of Azof. No dream of unity had come to anyone. But had there been a forecast then of the future, it would have been said that the more finely organized Finn would become the dominant race; or perhaps the Bulgarian, who was showing capacity for empire-building; but certainly not that helpless Slavonic people wedged in between their stronger neighbors.

But there were no large ambitions yet. It meant nothing to them that there was a new "Holy Roman Empire," and that Charlemagne had been crowned at Rome successor of the Roman Caesars (800 A. D.); nor that an England had just been consolidated into one kingdom. Nor did it concern them that the Saracen had overthrown a Gothic empire in Spain (710). For them these things did not exist. But they knew about Constantinople. The Byzantine Empire was the sun which shone beyond their horizon, and was for them the supreme type of power and earthly splendor. Whatever ambitions and aspirations would in time awaken in these Oriental breasts must inevitably have for their ideal the splendid despotism of the Eastern Caesars. But that stage had not yet been reached.

Although branches of the Slavonic race had separated from the parent stem, bearing different names, the Bohemians on the Vistula, the Poliani in what was to become Poland, the Lithuanians near the Baltic, and minor tribes scattered elsewhere, from the Peloponnesus to the Baltic, all had the same general characteristics. Their religion, like that of all Aryan peoples, was a pantheism founded upon the phenomena of nature. In their Pantheon there was a Volos, a solar deity who, like the Greek Apollo, was inspirer of poets and protector of the flocks—Perun, God of Thunder—Stribog, the father of the Winds, like Aeolus—a Proteus who could assume all shapes—Centaurs, Vampires, and hosts of minor deities, good and evil. There were neither temples nor priests, but the oak was venerated and consecrated to Perun; and rude idols of wood stood upon the hills, where sacrifices were offered to them and they were worshiped by the people.

They believed that their dead passed into a future life, and from the time of the early Scythians it had been the custom to strangle a male and a female servant of the deceased to accompany him on his journey to the other land. The barbarity of their religious rites varied with the different tribes, but the general characteristics were the same, and the people everywhere were profoundly attached to their pagan ceremonies and under the dominion of an intense form of superstition.

Slav society was everywhere founded upon the patriarchal principle. The father was absolute head of the family, his authority passing undiminished upon his death to the oldest surviving member. This was the social unit.

The Commune, or Mir, was only the expansion of the family, and was subject to the authority of a council, composed of the elders of the several families, called the vetché. The village lands were held in common by this association. The territory was the common property of the whole. No hay could be cut nor fish caught without permission from the vetché. Then all shared alike the benefit of the enterprise.

The communes nearest together formed a still larger group called a Volost; that is, a canton or parish, which was governed by a council composed of the elders of the communes, one of whom was recognized as the chief. Beyond this the idea of combination or unity did not extend. Such was the primitive form of society which was common to all the Slavonic branches. It was communistic, patriarchal, and just to the individual. They had no conception of tribal unity, nor of a sovereignty which should include the whole. If the Slav ever came under the despotism of a strong personal government, the idea must come from some external source; it must be imposed, not grow; for it was not indigenous in the character of the people. It would be perfectly natural for them to submit to it if it came, for they were a passive people, but they were incapable of creating it.

CHAPTER III.RURIK AND HIS DESCENDANTS

The Russian Slavs were an agricultural, not a warlike, people. They fought bravely, but naked to the waist, and with no idea of military organization, so were of course no match for the Turks, well skilled in the arts of war, nor for the armed bands of Scandinavian merchants, who made their territory a highway by which to reach the Greek provinces. All the Slav asked was to be permitted to gather his harvests, and dwell in his wooden towns and villages in peace. But this he could not do. Not only was he under tribute to the Khazarui (a powerful tribe of mingled Finnish and Turkish blood), and harried by the Turks, in the South; overrun by the Finns and Lithuanians in the North; but in his imperfect political condition he was broken up into minute divisions, canton incessantly at war with canton, and there could be no peace. The roving bands of Scandinavian traders and freebooters were alternately his persecutors and protectors. After burning his villages for some fancied offense, and appropriating his cattle and corn, they would sell their service for the protection of Kief, Novgorod, and Pskof as freely as they did the same thing to Constantinople and the Greek cities. In other words, these brilliant, masterful intruders were Northmen, and can undoubtedly be identified with those roving sea-kings who terrorized Western Europe for a long and dreary period.

The disheartened Slavs of Novgorod came to a momentous decision. They invited these Varangians—as they are called—to come and administer their government. They said: "Our land is great and fruitful, but it lacks order and justice. Come—take possession, and govern us." With the arrival from Sweden of the three Vikings, Rurik and his two brothers Sineus and Truvor, the true history of Russia begins, and the one thousandth anniversary of that event was commemorated at Novgorod in the year 1862.

Rurik was the Clovis of Russia. When with his band of followers he was established at Novgorod the name of Russia came into existence, supposedly from the Finnish word ruotsi, meaning rowers or sea-farers. Slavonia was not only christened but regenerated at this period, and infused into it were the new elements of martial order, discipline, and the habit of implicit obedience to a chosen or hereditary chief; and as Rurik's brothers soon conveniently died, their territory also passed to him, and he assumed the title of Grand Prince.

Upon the death of Rurik in 879, his younger brother Oleg succeeded him as regent during the minority of his son Igor; and when two more Varangian brothers—Askold and Dir—in the same manner—except that they were not invited—took possession of Kief on the Dnieper and set up a rival principality in the South with ambitious designs upon Byzantium, Oleg promptly had them assassinated, added their territory to the dominion of Igor, and removed the capital from Novgorod to Kief—saying, "Let Kief be the mother of Russian cities!" Then after selecting a wife named Olga for the young Igor, he turned his attention toward Byzantium, the powerful magnet about which Russian policy was going to revolve for many centuries.

So invincible and so wise was this Oleg that he was believed to be a sorcerer. When the Greek emperor blockaded the passage of the Bosphorus in 907, he placed his two thousand boats (!) upon wheels, and let the sails carry them overland to the gates of Constantinople. The Russian poet Pushkin has made this the subject of a poem which tells how Oleg, after exacting tribute from the frightened Emperor Leo VI., in true Norse fashion, hung his shield upon the golden gates as a parting insult.

Again and again were the Greeks compelled to pay for immunity from these invasions of the Varangian princes. After the death of Oleg, Igor reigned, and in 941 led another expedition against Constantinople which we are told was driven back by "Greek-fire." Then enlisting the aid of the Pechenegs, a ferocious Tatar tribe, he returned with such fury, and inflicted such atrocities, that the Greek Emperor begged for mercy and offered to pay any price to be left alone. The invaders said: "If Caesar speaks thus, what more do we want than to have gold and silver and silks without fighting." A treaty of peace was signed (945), the Russians swearing by their god Perun, and the Greeks by the Gospels; and the victorious Igor turned his face toward Kief. But he was never to reach that place.

The Drevlians, the most savage of the Tatar tribes, had been forced to pay him a large tribute, and were meditating upon their revenge. They said: "Let us kill the wolf or we will lose the flock." They watched their opportunity, seized him, tied him to two young trees bent forcibly together; then, letting them spring apart, the son of Rurik was torn to pieces.

No act of the wise regent Oleg was more fruitful in consequences than the choice of a wife for the young Igor. Olga, who acted as regent during the minority of her son, was destined to be not only the heroine of the Epic Cycle in Russia, but the first apostle of Christianity in that heathen land; canonized by the Church, and remembered as "the first Russian who mounted to the Heavenly Kingdom."

When the Drevlians sent gifts to appease her wrath at the murder of Igor, and offered her the hand of their prince, she had the messengers buried alive. All she asked was three pigeons and three sparrows from every house in their capital town. Lighted tow was tied to the tails of the birds, which were then permitted to fly back to their homes under the eaves of the thatched houses. In the conflagration which followed, the inhabitants were massacred in a pleasing variety of ways; some strangled, some smothered in vapor, some buried alive, and those remaining reduced to slavery.

But an extraordinary transformation was at hand; and this vindictive heathen woman was going to be changed to an ardent convert to the Christian faith. Nestor, who is the Russian Herodotus, relates that she went to Constantinople in 955, to inquire into the mysteries of the Christian Church. The emperor was astonished, it is said, at the strength and adroitness of her mind. She was baptized by the Greek Patriarch, under the new name of Helen, the emperor acting as her godfather.

There were already a few Christians in Kief, but so unpopular was the new religion that Olga's son Sviatoslaf, upon reaching his majority, absolutely refused to make himself ridiculous by adopting his mother's faith. "My men will mock me," was his reply to Olga's entreaties, and

Nestor adds "that he often became furious with her" for her importunity.

Sviatoslaf, the son of Igor and Olga, although the first prince to bear a Russian name, was the very type of the cunning, ambitious, and intrepid Northman, and his brief reign (964-972) displayed all these qualities. He defeated the Khazarui, the most civilized of all those Oriental people, and once the most powerful. He subjugated the Pechenegs, perhaps the most brutal and least civilized of all the barbarians. But these were only incidental to his real purpose.

The Bulgarian Empire was large, and had played an important part in the past. It had a Tsar, while Russia had only a Grand Prince, and, although now declining in strength, was a troublesome neighbor to the Greek Empire. The oft-repeated mistake of inviting the aid of another people was committed. Nothing could have better pleased Sviatoslaf than to assist the Greek Empire, and when he captured the Bulgarian capital city on the Danube, and even talked of making it his own capital instead of Kief, it looked as if a great Slav Empire was forming with its center almost within sight of Constantinople. The Greeks were dismayed. With the Russians in the Balkan Peninsula, the center of their dominions upon the Danube—with the Scythian hordes in the South ready to do their bidding—and with scattered Slavonic tribes from Macedon to the Peloponnesos gravitating toward them, what might they not do? No more serious danger had ever threatened the Empire of the East. They rushed to rescue Bulgaria from the very enemy they had invited to overthrow it. After a prolonged struggle, and in spite of the wild courage displayed by Sviatoslaf, he was driven back, and compelled to swear by Perun and Volos never again to invade Bulgaria. If they broke their vows, might they become "as yellow as gold, and perish by their own arms." But this was for Sviatoslaf the last invasion of any land. The avenging Pechenegs were waiting in ambush for his return. They cut off his head and presented his skull to their Prince as a drinking cup (972).

It seems scarcely necessary to call attention to the fact that the transforming energy in this early period of Russian history was not in the native people; but that the Slav, in the hands of his Norse rulers, was as clay in the hands of the potter. In the treaty of peace signed at Kief (945) by the victorious Igor, of the fifty names recorded by Nestor only three were Slavonic and the rest Scandinavian. There can be no doubt which was the dominant race in this the heroic age of Russia.

So we have seen a weaker people submitting to the rule of a stronger, not by conquest, like Spain under the Visigoths; not overrun and overridden as Britain by the Angles and Saxons and Gaul by the Franks; but, in recognition of its own helplessness, voluntarily becoming subject to the control of strangers.

And we see at the same time the brilliant, restless Norseman, with no plan of establishing a racial dominion, but simply in the temporary enjoyment of his own warlike and robber instincts, engrafting himself upon a less gifted people, and then adopting its language and customs, letting himself be absorbed into the nationality he has helped to create, and becoming a Russian, with the same facility as Rollo and his sons at the very same period were becoming Frenchmen.

CHAPTER IV.RUSSIANS CONVERSION—GREEK AND LATIN CHRISTIANITY

So the scattered clans of the Slav race were roughly drawn together into something resembling a nation by the strong arm of the Scandinavian. But the course of national progress is never a straight one. Nature understands better than we the value of retarding influences, which prevent the too rapid fusing of crude elements. This work of retardation was performed for Russia by Sviatoslaf. When, instead of leaving his dominions to his oldest son, he divided them among the three, he introduced a vicious system which was to become a fatal source of weakness. This is known as the system of Appanages. To his son Yaropolk he gave Kief, to Oleg the territory of the Drevlians, and to Vladimir Novgorod. But as Vladimir quickly assassinated Yaropolk, who had already assassinated Oleg, the injurious results of the system were not directly felt!

Vladimir became the sole ruler. He then started upon a course of unbridled profligacy. He compelled the widow of his murdered brother to marry him—then a beautiful Greek nun who had been captured from Byzantium—then a Bulgarian and a Bohemian wife, until finally his household was numbered by hundreds. But this sensual barbarian began to be conscious of a soul. He was troubled, and revived the worship of the Slav gods; erected on the cliffs near Kief a new idol of Perun, with head of silver and beard of gold. Two Scandinavian Christians were by his orders stabbed at the feet of the idol. Still his soul was unsatisfied. He determined upon a search for the best religion; sent ambassadors to examine into the religious beliefs of Mussulmans, Jews, Catholics, and the Greeks. The splendor of the Greek ceremonial, the magnificence of the vestments, the incense, the music, and the presence of the Emperor and his court, filled the souls of the barbarians with awe—and the final argument of his boyars (or nobles) put an end to doubts: "If the Greek religion had not been the best, your grandmother Olga, the wisest of mortals, would not have adopted it."

Vladimir's choice was made. He would be baptized in the faith of Olga. But this must be done at the hand of the Greek Patriarch; so he would conquer baptism—and ravish it like booty—not beg for it. He besieged and took a Greek city. Then demanded the hand of Anna, sister of the Greek Caesar, threatening in case of refusal to march on Constantinople. Consent was given upon condition of baptism, which was just what the barbarian wanted. So he came back to Kief a Christian, bringing with him his new Greek wife, and his new baptismal name of Basil.

Amid the tears and fright of the people, the idols were torn down; Perun was flogged and thrown into the Dnieper. Then the old pagan stream was consecrated, and men, women, and children, old and young, master and slave, were driven into the river, the Greek priests standing on the banks reading the baptismal service. The frightened Novgorodians were in like manner forced to hurl Perun into the Volkhof, and then, like herded cattle, were driven into the stream to be baptized. The work of Olga was completed—Russia was Christianized (992)!

It would be long before Christianity would penetrate into the heart of the people. As late as the twelfth century only the higher classes faithfully observed the Christian rites; while the old pagan ceremonies were still common among the peasantry. And even now the Saints of the Calendar are in some places only thinly disguised heathen deities and pagan rites and superstitions mingle with Christian observances.

The conversion of Vladimir seems to have been sincere. From being a cruel voluptuary and assassin, he was changed to a merciful ruler who could not bear to inflict capital punishment. He was faithful to his Greek wife Anna. On the spot where he had once erected Perun, and where the two Scandinavians were martyred at his command, he built the church of St. Basil; and he is now remembered only as the saint who Christianized pagan Russia, and revered as the "Beautiful Sun of Kief."

So the two most important events considered thus far in the history of this land have been, first, its military conquest from the North, and second, its ecclesiastical conquest from the South. If the first helped it to become a nation, the second determined the character which that nationality should assume.

To explain one fact by another and unfamiliar and uncomprehended fact is one of the confusing methods of history! In order to know why the adoption of the form of religion known as the Greek Church so powerfully influenced Russian development, one must understand what that faith was and is, and the source of the antagonisms which divided the two great branches of the Church of Christ—the Greek and the Latin.

The cause underlying all others is racial. It is explained in their names. The theology of one had its roots in Greek Philosophy; that of the other in Roman Law. One tended to a brilliant diversity, the other to centralization and unity. One was a group of Ecclesiastical States, a Hierarchy and a Polyarchy, governed by Patriarchs, each supreme in his own diocese; the other was a Monarchy, arbitrarily and diplomatically governed from one center. It was the difference between an archipelago and a continent, and not unlike the difference between ancient Greece and Rome. One had the tremendous principle of growth, stability, and permanence; the other had not.

Such were the race tendencies which led to entirely different ecclesiastical systems. Then there arose differences in dogma; and Rome considered the Church in the East schismatic, and Byzantium held that that of the West was heterodox. They now not only disapproved of each other's methods, but what was more serious, held different creeds. The Latin Church, after its Bishop had become an infallible Pope (about the middle of the fifth century), claimed that the Church in the East must accept his definition of dogma as final.

It was one small word which finally rent these two bodies of Christendom forever apart. It was only the word filioque which made the impassable gulf dividing them. The Latins maintained that the Holy Spirit proceeded from the Father—and the son; the Greeks that it descended from the Father alone. It was the undying controversy concerning the relations and the attributes of the three Members of the Trinity; and the insoluble question was destined to break up Greek and

Catholic Church alike into numberless sects and shades of belief or unbelief; and over this Christological controversy, rivers of blood were to flow in both branches of Christendom.

The theological question involved was of course too subtle for ordinary comprehension. But although men on both sides stood ready to die for the decisions of their councils which they did not understand, there was underlying the whole question the political jealousy existing between the two: Byzantium, embittered by the effacement of its political jurisdiction in the West, exasperated at the overweening pretensions of Roman bishops; Rome, watching for opportunity to cajole or compel the Eastern Church to submit to her authority and headship.

Such was the condition of things when Russia allied herself in that most vital way with the empire in the East. It is impossible to measure the importance of the step, or to imagine what would have been the history of that country had Vladimir decided to accept the religion of Rome and become Catholic, as the Slav in Poland had already done. By his choice not only is it possible that he added some centuries to the life of the Greek Empire itself, but he determined the type of Russian civilization. When she allied herself with Byzantium instead of Rome, Russia separated herself from those European currents from which she was already by natural and inherited conditions isolated. She thus prolonged and emphasized the Orientalism which so largely shaped her destiny, and produced a nationality absolutely unique in the family of European nations, in that there is but one single root in Russia which can be traced back to the Roman Empire; and whereas most of the European civilizations are built upon a Roman foundation, there is only one current in the life of that nation to-day which has flowed from a Latin source: that is a judicial code which was founded (in part) upon Roman law as embodied by Justinian, Emperor of the Empire in the East (527-565).

CHAPTER V. PRINCIPALITIES— EXPANSION NORTHWARD

When Vladimir died, in 1015, the partition of his dominions among numerous heirs inaugurated the destructive system of Appanages. The country was converted into a group of principalities ruled by Princes of the same blood, of which the Principality of Kief was chief, and its ruler Grand Prince. Kief, the "Mother of Cities," was the heart of Russia, and its Prince, the oldest of the descendants of Rurik, had a recognized supremacy over the others; who must, however, also belong to this royal line. No prince could rule anywhere who was not a descendant of Rurik; Kief, the greatest prize of all, going to the oldest; and when a Grand Prince died, his son was not his rightful heir, but his uncle, or brother, or cousin, or whoever among the Princes had the right by seniority. This was a survival of the patriarchal system of the Slavs, showing how the Norse rulers had adapted themselves to the native customs as before stated.

So while in thus breaking up the land into small jealous and rival states independent of each other—with only a nominal headship at Kief—while in this there was a movement toward chaos, there were after all some bonds of unity which could not be severed: A unity of race and language; a unity of historical development; a unity in religion; and the political unity created by the fact that all the thrones were filled by members of the same family, any one of whom might become Grand Prince if enough of the intervening members could—by natural or other means— be disposed of. This was a standing invitation for assassination and anarchy, and one which was not neglected.

Immediately upon the death of Vladimir there commenced a carnival of fraternal murders, which ended by leaving Yaroslaf to whom had been assigned the Principality of Novgorod, upon the throne at Kief.

The "Mother of Russian Cities" began to show the effect of Greek influences. The Greek clergy had brought something besides Oriental Christianity into the land of barbarians. They brought a desire for better living. Learning began to be prized; schools were created. Music and architecture, hitherto absolutely unknown, were introduced. Kief grew splendid, and with its four hundred churches and its gilded cupolas lighted by the sun, was striving to be like Constantinople. Not alone the Sacred Books of Byzantine literature, but works upon philosophy and science, and even romance, were translated into the Slavonic language. Russia was no longer the simple, untutored barbarian, guided by unbridled impulses. She was taking her first lesson in civilization. She was beginning to be wise; learning new accomplishments, and, alas!—to be systematically and judicially cruel!

Nothing could have been more repugnant or foreign to the free Slav barbarian than the penal code which was modeled by Yaroslaf upon the one at Byzantium. Corporal punishment was unknown to the Slav, and was abhorrent to his instincts. This seems a strange statement to make regarding the land of the knout! But it is true. And imprisonment, convict labor, flogging, torture, mutilation, and even the death penalty, came into this land by the way of Constantinople.

At the same time there mingled with this another stream from Scandinavia, another judicial code which sanctioned private revenge, the pursuit of an assassin by all the relatives of the dead; also the ordeal by red-hot iron and boiling water. But to the native Slav race, corporal punishment, with its humiliations and its refinements of cruelty, was unknown until brought to it by stronger and wiser people from afar.

When we say that Russia was putting on a garment of civilization, let no one suppose we mean the people of Russia. It was the Princes, and their military and civil households; it was official Russia that was doing this. The people were still sowing and reaping, and sharing the fruit of their toil in common, unconscious as the cattle in their fields that a revolution was taking place, ready to be driven hither and thither, coerced by a power which they did not comprehend, their horizon bounded by the needs of the day and hour.

The elements constituting Russian society were the same in all the principalities. There was first the Prince. Then his official family, a band of warriors called the Drujina. This Drujina was the germ of the future state. Its members were the faithful servants of the Prince, his guard and his counselors. He could constitute them a court of justice, or could make them governors of fortresses (posadniki) or lieutenants in the larger towns. The Prince and his Drujina were like a family of soldiers, bound together by a close tie. The body was divided into three orders of rank: first, the simple guards; second, those corresponding to the French barons; and, third, the Boyars, the most illustrious of all, second only to the Prince. The Drujina was therefore the germ of aristocratic Russia, next below it coming the great body of the people, the citizens and traders, then the peasant, and last of all the slave.

Yaroslaf, the "legislator," known as the Charlemagne of Russia, died in the year 1054. The Eastern and Western Empires, long divided in sentiment, were that same year separated in fact, when Pope Leo VI. excommunicated the whole body of the Church in the East.

With the death of Yaroslaf the first and heroic period in Russia closes. Sagas and legendary poems have preserved for us its grim outlines and its heroes, of whom Vladimir, the "Beautiful Sun of Kief," is chief. Thus far there has been a unity in the thread of Russian history—but now came chaos. Who can relate the story of two centuries in which there have been 83 civil wars— 18 foreign campaigns against one country alone, not to speak of the others—46 barbaric invasions, and in which 293 Princes are said to have disputed the throne of Kief and other domains! We repeat: Who could tell this story of chaos; and who, after it is told, would read it?

It was a vast upheaval, a process in which the eternal purposes were "writ large"—too large to be read at the time. It was not intended that only the fertile Black Lands along the Dnieper, near to the civilizing center at Constantinople, should absorb the life currents. All of Russia was to be vitalized; the bleak North as well as the South; the zone of the forests as well as the fertile steppes. The instruments appointed to accomplish this great work were—the disorder consequent upon the reapportionment of the territory at the death of each sovereign—the fierce rivalries of ambitious Princes—and the barbaric encroachments to which the prevailing anarchy made the South the prey.

By the twelfth century the civil war had become distinctly a war between a new Russia of the forests and the old Russia of the fertile steppes. The cause of the North had a powerful leader in Andrew Bogoliubski. Andrew was the grandson of Monomakh and the son of Yuri (or George) Dolgoruki—both of whom were Grand Princes of extraordinary abilities and commanding qualities. In 1169 Andrew, who was then Prince of Suzdal, came with an immense army of followers; he marched against Kief. The "Mother of Russian Cities" was taken by assault, sacked and pillaged, and the Grand Principality ceased to exist. Russia was preparing to revolve around a new center in the Northeast; and with the new Grand Principality of Suzdal, far removed from Byzantine and Western civilizations, it looked like a return toward barbarism, but was in fact the circuitous road to progress. The life of the nation needed to be drawn to its extremities, and the ambitious Andrew, who assumed the title and authority of Grand Prince, had established a line which was destined to lead to the Czars of future Russia.

CHAPTER VI.GERMAN INVASION— MONGOL INVASION

The Principality of Novgorod had from a remote antiquity been the political center of Northern, as was Kief of Southern Russia. It was the Novgorodians who invited the Norse Princes to come and rule the land; and it was the Novgorodians who were their least submissive subjects. When one of the Grand Princes proposed to send his son, whom they did not want, to be their Prince, they replied: "Send him here if he has a spare head." It was a fearless, proud republic, as patriotic and as quarrelsome as Florence, which it somewhat resembled. Their Prince was in reality a figurehead. He was considered essential to the dignity of the state, but his fortunes were in the hands of two political parties, of which he represented the party in the ascendant. Novgorod was a commercial city—its life was in its trade with the Orient and the Greek Empire, and like the Italian cities, its politics were swayed by economic interests. Those in trade with the East through the Volga desired a Prince from one of the great families about that Oriental artery in the Southeast; while those whose fortunes depended upon the Greeks preferred one from Kief or the principalities on the Dnieper. When one party fell, the Prince fell with it, and as the formula expressed it, they then "made him a reverence, and showed him the way out of Novgorod"—or else held him captive until his successor arrived.

Princes might come, and Princes might go, but an irrepressible spirit of freedom "went on forever"; the reigns all too short and troubled to disturb the ancient liberties and customs of the republic. No Grand Prince was ever powerful enough to impose upon them a Prince they did not want, and no Prince strong enough to oppose the will of the people; every act of his requiring the sanction of their posadnik, a high official—and every decision subject to reversal by the Vetché, the popular assembly. The Vetché was, in fact, the real sovereign of the proud republic which styled itself, "My Lord Novgorod the Great." Such was the remarkable state which played an important, and certainly the most picturesque, part in the history of Russia.

The first thought of the new Grand Prince at Suzdal was to prevent the possible rivalry of this arrogant principality in the North, by conquering it and breaking its spirit. He was also resolved to break thoroughly with the past, to destroy the system of Appanages, and had conceived the idea of the modern undivided state. He removed his capital from the old town of Suzdal, which had its Vetché or popular assembly, to Vladimir, which had had none of these things, assigning as his reason, not that he intended to be sole master and free from all ancient trammels—but that the Mother of God had come to him in a dream and commanded him so to do! But an end came to all his dreams and ambitions. He was assassinated in 1174 by his own boyars, who were exasperated by his subversive policy and suspicions of his daring reforms.

With the setting of the currents of Russian national life toward the North, there was awakened in Europe a vague sense of danger. Not far from Novgorod, on and about the shores of the Baltic, were various tributary Slav tribes, mingled with pagan Finns. This was the only point of actual contact, the only point without natural protection between Russia and Europe, and it must be guarded. German merchants, hand in hand with Latin missionaries, invaded a strip of disputed territory, and, under the cloak of Christianity, commenced a—conquest. A Latin Church became also a fortress; and the fortress soon expanded into a German town, and these crept every year farther and farther into the East. In order to quell the resistance of native Finns and Slavs, there was created, and authorized by the Pope, an order of knighthood, called the "Sword-Bearers," with the double purpose of driving back the Slavonic tide which threatened Germany and at the same time Christianizing it. These were the "Livonian Knights," who came from Saxony and Westphalia, armed cap-à-pie, with red crosses embroidered upon the shoulder of their white mantles. Then another order was created (1225), the "Teutonic Order," wearing black crosses on their shoulders, which, after fraternizing with the Livonian Knights, was going to absorb them— together with some other things—into their own more powerful organization. Russia had no armed warriors to meet these steel-clad Germans and Livonians. She had no orders of chivalry, had taken no part in the Crusades, the far-off echoes of which had fallen upon unheeding ears. The Russians could defend with desperate courage their own flimsy fortifications of wood, earth, and loose stones; but they could not pull down with ropes the solid German fortresses of stone and cement, and their spears were ineffectual upon the shining armor. Their conquest was inevitable; the conquered territory being divided between the knights and the Latin Church. So Königsberg and many other Russian towns were captured and then Teutonized, by joining them to the cities of Lubeck, Bremen, Hamburg, etc., in the "Hanseatic League."

This conquest was of less future importance to Russia than to Western Europe. It contained the germ of much history. The territory thus wrested from Russia became the German state of Prussia; and a future master of the Teutonic order, a Hohenzollern, was in later years its first King; and this was the beginning of the great German Empire which confronts the Empire of the Czar to-day.

So the conquest by the German Orders was added to the other woes by which Russia was rent and torn after the death of her Grand Prince at Suzdal. To us it all seems like an unmeaning panorama of chaos and disorder. But to them it was only the vicissitudes naturally occurring in the life of a great nation. They were proud of their nationality, which had existed nearly as long as from Columbus to our own day. They gloried in their splendid background of great deeds and their long line of heroes reaching back to Rurik. Their Princes were proud and powerful—their followers (the Drujiniki)—noble and fearless—who could stand before them? They would have exchanged their glories for those of no nation upon the earth, except perhaps that waning empire of the Caesars at Constantinople!

Such was the sentiment of Russian nationality at the time when its overwhelming humiliation suddenly came, a degrading subjection to Asiatic Mongols, which lasted 250 years.

In the year 1224 there appeared in the Southeast a strange host who claimed the land of the Polovtsui, a Tatar clan which had been for centuries encamped about the Sea of Azof. The Russian chronicler naively says: "There came upon us for our sins unknown nations. God alone knew who they were, or where they came from—God, and perhaps wise men, learned in books"—which it is evident the chronicler was not! The invaders were Mongols—that branch of the human family from which had come the Tatars and the Huns, already familiar to Russia. But these Mongols were the vanguard of a vast army which had streamed like a torrent through the heart of Asia, conquering as it came; gathering one after another the Asiatic kingdoms into an empire ruled by Genghis Khan, a sovereign who in forty years had made himself master of China and the greater part of Asia—saying: "As there is only one Sun in Heaven, so there should be only one Emperor on the Earth"; and when he died, in 1227, he left the largest empire that had ever existed, and one which he was preparing to extend into Western Europe.

It was the court of this great sovereign which, in 1275, was visited by the Venetian traveler Marco Polo. This was the far-off Cathay, descriptions of which fired the imagination of Europe, and awoke a consuming desire to get access to its fabulous riches, and which two centuries later filled the mind of Columbus with dreams of reaching that land of wonders by way of the West.

The Polovtsui appealed to the nearest principalities for help, offering to adopt their religion and to become their subjects, in return for aid. When several Princes came with their armies to the rescue, the Mongols sent messengers saying: "We have no quarrel with you; we have come to destroy the accursed Polovtsui." The Princes replied by promptly putting the ambassadors all to death. This sealed the fate of Russia. There could be no compromise after that. Upon that first battlefield, on the steppes near the sea of Azof, there were left six Princes, seventy chief boyars, and all but one-tenth of the Russian army.

After this thunderbolt had fallen an ominous quiet reigned for thirteen years. Nothing more was heard of the Mongols—but a comet blazing in the sky awoke vague fears. Suddenly an army of five hundred thousand Asiatics returned, led by Batui, nephew of the Great Khan of Khans.

It was the defective political structure of Russia, its division into principalities, which made it an easy prey. The Mongols, moving as one man, took one principality at a time, its nobles and citizens alone bearing arms, the peasants, by far the greater part, being utterly defenseless. After wrecking and devastating that, they passed on to the next, which, however desperately defended, met the same fate. The Grand Principality was a ruin; its fourteen towns were burned, and when, in the absence of its Grand Prince, Vladimir the capital city fell, the Princesses and all the families of the nobles took refuge in the cathedral and perished in the general conflagration (1238). Two years later Kief also fell, with its white walls and towers embellished by Byzantine art, its cupolas of gold and silver. All was laid in the dust, and only a few fragments in museums now remain to tell of its glory. The annalist describes the bellowings of the buffaloes, the cries of the camels, the neighing of the horses, and howlings of the Tatars while the ancient and beautiful city was being laid low.

Before 1240 the work was complete. There was a Mongol empire where had been a Russian. Then the tide began to set toward Western Europe. Isolated from the other European states by her religion, Russia had suffered alone. No Europe sprang to her defense as to the defense of Spain from the Saracens. Not until Poland and Hungary were threatened and invaded did the Western Kingdoms give any sign of interest. Then the Pope, in alarm, appealed to the Christian states. Frederick II. of Germany responded, and Louis IX. of France (Saint-Louis) prepared to lead a crusade. But the storm had spent its fury upon the Slavonic people, and was content to pause upon those plains which to the Asiatic seemed not unlike his own home.

CHAPTER VII.UNDER MONGOL YOKE

Amid the wreck of principalities there was one state remaining erect. Novgorod was defended by its remoteness and its uninviting climate. The Mongols had not thought it worth while to attempt the reduction of the warlike state, so the stalwart Republic stood alone amid the general ruin. All the rest were under the Tatar yoke. Of Princes there were none. All had either been slaughtered or fled. Proud boyars saw their wives and daughters the slaves of barbarians. Delicate women who had always lived in luxury were grinding corn and preparing coarse food for their terrible masters.

After the conquest was completed the Mongol sovereign exacted only three things from the prostrate state—homage, tribute, and a military contingent when required. They might retain their land and their customs, might worship any god in any way; their Princes might dispute for the thrones as before; but no Prince—not the Grand Prince himself—could ascend a throne until he had permission from the Great Khan, to whom also every dispute between royal claimants must be deferred. Then when finally the messenger came from the sovereign with the yarlik, or royal sanction, the Prince must listen kneeling, with his head in the dust. And if then he was invited (?) to the Mongol court to pay homage, he must go, even though it required (as Marco Polo tells us) four years to make the journey across the plains and the mountains and rivers and the Great Desert of Gobi!

When Yaroslaf II., third Grand Prince of Suzdal, succeeded to the Principality, he was invited to pay this visit. After reaching there, and after all the degrading ceremonies to which he was subjected—kissing the stirrup of his Suzerain, and licking up the drops which fell from his cup as he drank—then this Prince of the family of Rurik perished from exhaustion in the Desert of Gobi on his return journey. But this was not all. The yoke was a heavy as well as a degrading one. Each Prince with his Drujina must be always ready to lead an army in defense of the Mongol cause if required; and, last of all, the poll-tax bore with intolerable weight upon everyone, rich or poor, excepting only the ecclesiastics and the property of the Greek Church, which with a singular clemency they exempted.

What sort of a despotism was it, and what sort of a being, that could wield such a power from such a distance! that, across a continent it took four years to traverse, could compel such obedience; could by a word or a nod bring proud Princes with rage and rebellion in their hearts to his court—not to be honored and enriched, but degraded and insulted; then in shame to turn back with their boyars and retinues,—if indeed they were permitted to go back at all,—one-half of whom would perish from exhaustion by the way. What was the secret of such a power? Even with all the modern appliances for conveying the will of a sovereign to-day, with railroads to carry his messengers and telegraph wires to convey his will, would it be conceivable to exert such an authority?

And—listen to the language of a proud Russian Prince at the Court of the Great Khan: "Lord—all-powerful Tsar, if I have done aught against you, I come hither to receive life or death. I am ready for either. Do with me as God inspires you." Or still another: "My Lord and master, by thy mercy hold I my principality—with no title but thy protection and investiture—thy yarlik; while my uncle claims it not by your favor but by right!" It was such pleading as this that succeeded; so it is easy to see how Princes at last vied with each other in being abject. In this particular case the presumptuous uncle was ordered to lead his victorious nephew's horse by the bridle, on his way to his coronation at Moscow. So the path to success was through the dust, and it was the wily Princes of Moscow that most patiently traveled that road with important results to Russia.

Novgorod, as we have said, had alone escaped from these degradations. Her Prince Alexander was son of Yaroslaf, the Grand Prince who perished in the desert on his way home. At the time of the invasion Alexander was leading an army against the Swedes and the Livonian Knights in defense of his Baltic provinces. It was Latin Christianity versus Greek, and by a great victory upon the banks of the Neva he earned undying fame and the surname of Nevski. Alexander Nevski is remembered as the hero of the Neva and of the North; yet even he was finally compelled to grovel at the feet of the barbarians. Novgorod alone had stood erect, had paid no tribute and offered no homage to the Khan. At last, when its destruction was at hand, thirty-six years after the invasion, Nevski had the heroism to submit to the inevitable. He advised a surrender. It needed a soul of iron to brave the indignation of the republic. "He offers us servitude!" they cried. The Posadnik who conveyed the counsel to the Vetché was murdered on the spot. But Alexander persisted, and he prevailed. His own son refused to share his father's disgrace, and left the state. Again and again the people withdrew the consent they had given. Better might Novgorod perish! But finally, when Alexander Nevski declared that he would go, that he would leave them to their fate, they yielded, and the Mongols came into a silent city, passing from house to house making lists of the inhabitants who must pay tribute.

Then the unhappy Prince went to prostrate himself before the Khan at Saraï. But his heart had broken with his spirit. He had saved his state, but the task had been too heavy for him. He died from exhaustion on his journey home (1260).

On account of internal convulsions in the Great Tatar Empire, now united by Kublai-Khan, the fourth in succession from Genghis-Khan, the Golden-Horde had separated from the parent state, and its Khan was absolute ruler of Russia. So from this time the ceremony of investiture was performed at Saraï; and the humiliating pilgrimages of the Princes were made to that city.

The religion of the Mongols at the time of the invasion was a paganism founded upon sorcery and magic; but they soon thereafter adopted Islamism, and became ardent followers of the Prophet (1272). Although they never attempted to Tatarize Russia, 250 years of occupation could not fail to leave indelible traces upon a civilization which was even more than before Orientalized. The dress of the upper classes became more Eastern—the flowing caftan replaced the tunic, the blood of the races mingled to some extent; even the Princes and boyars contracting marriages with Mongol women, so that in some of the future sovereigns the blood of the Tatar was to be mingled with that of Rurik.

A weaker nation would have been crushed and disheartened by such calamities as have been described. But Russia was not weak. She had a tremendous store of vigor for good or for evil.

Life had always been a terrible conflict, with nature and with man, and when there had been no other barbarians to fight, they had fought each other. Every muscle and every sinew had always been in the highest state of activity, and was toughened and strong, with an inextinguishable vitality. Such nations do not waste time in sentimental regrets. Their wounds, like those of animals, heal quickly, and they are urged on by a sort of instinct to wear out the chains they cannot break. By the time Novgorod came under the Tatar yoke the entire state had adjusted itself to its condition of servitude. Its internal economy was re-established, the peasants, in their Mirs or communes, sowed and reaped, and the people bought and sold, only a little more patient and submissive than before. The burden had grown heavier, but it must be borne and the tribute paid. The Princes, with wits sharpened by conflict, fought as they always had, with uncles, cousins, and brothers for the thrones; and then governed with a severity as nearly as possible like the one imposed upon themselves by their own master—the Great Khan.

The germ of future Russia was there; a strong, patient, toiling people firmly held by a despotic power which they did not comprehend, and uncomplainingly and as a matter of course giving nearly one-half of the fruit of their toil for the privilege of living in their own land! When her sovereigns had Tatar blood in their veins and Tatar ideals in their hearts, Russia was on the road to absolutism. All things were tending toward a centralized unity of an iron and inexorable type—a type entirely foreign to the natural free instincts of the Slavonic people themselves.

CHAPTER VIII. RUSSIA BECOMES MUSCOVITE

The tumultuous forces in Russia, never at rest, were preparing to revolve about a new center. Whether this would be in the East or West was long in doubt, and only decided after a prolonged struggle. Western Russia grouped itself about the state of the Lithuanians on the Baltic, and Eastern Russia about that of Muscovy.

The Lithuanians had never been Christianized; they still adored Perun and their pagan deities; and the only bond uniting them with Russia was the tribute they had for years reluctantly paid. They were ripe for rebellion; and when after long years of conflict with the Livonian and Teutonic Orders, Latin Christianity obtained some foothold in their land, they began to gravitate toward Catholic Poland instead of Greek Russia; and when a marriage was suggested which should unite Poland and Lithuania under their Prince Iagello, who should reign over both at Cracow, and at the same time give them their own Grand Prince, they consented. The forces instigating this movement had their source at Rome, where the Pope was unceasingly striving, through Germany and Poland, to carry the Latin cross into Russia. Again and again had the Greek Church repulsed the offers of reconciliation and union made by Rome. So, much was hoped from the proselyting of the German Orders, and of Catholic Poland, and from the union effected by the marriage of the Lithuanian Prince Iagello with the Polish Queen Hedwig.

The threads composing this network of policies in the West were altogether ecclesiastical, until Lithuania began to feel strong enough to wash off her Christian baptism and to indulge in ambitious designs of her own: to struggle away from Poland, and to commence an independent and aggressive movement against Russia.

There was an immense vigor in this movement. The power in the West, sometimes Catholic and at heart always pagan, absorbed first towns and cities and then principalities. It began to be a Lithuanian conquest, and overshadowed even Mongol oppression. The Mongol wanted tribute; while Lithuania wanted Russia! But one of the gravest dangers brought by this war between the East and the West was the standing opportunity it offered to conspirators. An army of disaffected uncles and nephews and brothers, with their followers, could always find a refuge, and were always plotting and intriguing and negotiating with Lithuania and Poland, ready even to compromise their faith, if only they might ruin the existing powers.

Such, in brief, was the great conflict between the East and West, during which Moscow came into being as the supreme head, the living center and germ of Russian autocracy.

It seems to have been the extraordinary vitality of one family which twice changed the currents of national life: first drawing them from Kief to Suzdal, then from Suzdal toward Moscow, and there establishing a center of growth which has expanded into Russia as it exists to-day. This was the family of Dolgoruki. Monomakh and his son George Dolgoruki, the last Grand Prince of Kief, were both men of commanding character and abilities; and it will be remembered that it was Andrew Bogoliubski, the son of George (or Yuri), who effected the revolution which transferred the Grand Principality from Kief to Suzdal in the bleak North. Alexander Nevski, the hero of the Neva and of Novgorod, was the descendant of this Andrew (of Suzdal), and it was the son of Nevski who was the first Prince of Moscow and who there established a line of Princes which has come unbroken down to Nicholas II. Contrary to all the traditions of their state this dominating family was going to establish a dynasty, and again to remove the national life to a new center, in a Grand Principality toward which all of Russia was gradually but inevitably to gravitate until it became Muscovite.

The city which was to exert such an influence upon Russia was founded in 1147 by George (or Yuri) Dolgoruki, the last Grand Prince of Kief. The story is that upon arriving once at the domain of a boyar named Kutchko, he caused him for some offense to be put to death; then, as he looked out upon the river Moskwa from the height where now stands the Kremlin, so pleased was he with the outlook that he then and there planted the nucleus of a town. Whether the death of the boyar or the purpose of appropriating the domain came first, is not stated; but upon the soil freshly sprinkled with human blood arose Moscow.

The town was of so little importance that its destruction by the Tatars in 1238 was unobserved. In 1260, when Alexander Nevski died, Moscow, with a few villages, was given as a small appanage or portion to his son Daniel. Nevski, it must be remembered, was a direct descendant of Monomakh, and of George Dolgoruki, the founder of Moscow. So the first Prince of Moscow was of this illustrious line, a line which has remained unbroken until the present time.

When Daniel commenced to reign over what was probably the most obscure and insignificant principality in all Russia, it was surrounded by old and powerful states, in perpetual struggle with each other. The Lithuanian conquest was pressing in from the West and assuming large proportions; while embracing the whole agitated surface was the odious enslavement to the Mongols and their oft-recurring invasions to enforce their insolent demands.

The building of the Russian Empire was not a dainty task! It was not to be performed by delicate instruments and gentle hands. It needed brutal measures and unpitying hearts. Nor could brute force and cruelty do it alone; it required the subtler forces of mind—cold, calculating policies, patience, and craft of a subtle sort. The Princes of Russia had long been observant pupils, first at Constantinople, and later at the feet of the Khans. They could meet cruelty with cruelty, cunning with cunning. But it was the Princes of Moscow who proved themselves masters in these Oriental arts. Their cunning was not of the vulgar sort which works for ends that are near; it was the cunning which could wait, could patiently cringe and feign loyalty and devotion, with the steady purpose of tearing in pieces. Added to this, they had the intelligence to divine the secret of power. Certain ends they kept steadily in view. The old law of succession to eldest collateral heir they set aside from the outset; the principality being invariably divided among the sons of the deceased Prince. Then they gradually established the habit of giving to the eldest son Moscow, and only insignificant portions to the rest. So primogeniture lay at the root of the policy of the new state—and they had created a dynasty.

Then their invariable method was by cunning arts to embroil neighboring Princes in quarrels, and so to ingratiate themselves with their master the Khan, that when they appeared before him at Saraï—as they must—for his decision, while one unfortunate Prince (unless perchance he was beheaded and did not come away at all) came away without his throne, the faithful Prince of Moscow returned with a new state added to his territory and a new title to his name! Was he not always ready, not only to obey himself, but to enforce the obedience of others? Did he not stand ready to march against Novgorod, or any proud, refractory state which failed in tribute or homage to his master the Khan? No gloomier, no darker chapter is written in history than that which records the transition of Russia into Muscovy. It was rooted in a tragedy, it was nourished by human blood at every step of its growth. It was by base servility to the Khans, by perfidy to their peers, by treachery and by prudent but pitiless policy, that Moscow rose from obscurity to the supreme headship—and the name of Muscovy was attained.

There was a line of eight Muscovite Princes from Daniel (1260) to the death of Vasili (1462), but they moved as steadily toward one end as if one man had been during those two centuries guiding the policy of the state. The city of Moscow was made great. The Kremlin was built (1300)—not as we see it now. It required many centuries to accumulate all the treasures within that sacred inclosure of walls, crowned by eighteen towers. But with each succeeding reign there arose new buildings, more and more richly adorned by jewels and by Byzantine art.

Then the city became the ecclesiastical center of Russia, when the Metropolitan, second only to the Great Patriarch at Constantinople, was induced to remove to Moscow from Vladimir, capital of the Grand Principality. This was an important advance; for in the train of the great ecclesiastic came splendor of ritual, and wealth and culture and art; and a cathedral and more palaces must be added to the Kremlin. In 1328 Ivan I., the Prince of Moscow, being the eldest descendant of Rurik, fell heir by the old law of succession to the Grand Principality. So now the Prince of Moscow was also Grand Prince of Vladimir, or of Suzdal, which was the same thing; and as he continued to dwell in his own capital, the Grand Principality was ruled from Moscow. The first act of this Grand Prince was to claim sovereignty over Novgorod. The people were deprived of their Vetché and their posadnik, while one of his own boyars represented his authority and ruled as their Prince. Then the compliant Khan bestowed upon his faithful vassal the triple crown of Vladimir, Moscow, and Novgorod, to which were soon to be added many others.

The next step was to be the setting aside of the old Slavonic law of inheritance, and claiming the throne of the Grand Principality for the oldest son of the last reigning Grand Prince; making sure at the same time that this Prince belonged to the Muscovite line. This was not entirely accomplished until 1431, when Vasili carried his dispute to the Horde for the Khan's decision. The other disputant, who was making a desperate stand for his rights under the old system of seniority, was the "presumptuous uncle" already mentioned, who was, it will be remembered, commanded to lead by the bridle the horse of his triumphant Muscovite nephew. The sons of the disappointed uncle, however, conspired with success even after that; and finally, in a rage, Vasili ordered that the eyes of one of his cousins be put out. But time brings its revenges. Ten years later the Grand Prince, on an evil day, fell into the hands of the remaining cousin,—brother of his victim,—and had his own eyes put out. So he was thereafter known as "Vasili the Blind." This wily Prince kept his oldest son Ivan close to him; and, that there might be no doubt about his succession, so familiarized him with his position and placed him so firmly in the saddle that it would not be easy to unseat him when his own death occurred.

Many things had been happening during these two centuries besides the absorption of the Russian principalities by Moscow. The ambitious designs of Lithuania, in which Poland and Hungary, and the German Knights and Latin Christianity, were all involved, had been checked, and the disappointed state of Lithuania was gravitating toward a union with Poland. More important still, the Empire of the Khan was falling into pieces. The process had been hastened by a tremendous victory obtained by the Grand Prince Dmitri in 1378, on the banks of the Don. In the same way that Alexander Nevski obtained the surname of Nevski by the battle on the Neva, so Dmitri Donskoi won his upon the river Don. Hitherto the Tatars had been resisted, but not attacked. It was the first real outburst against the Mongol yoke, and it shook the foundations of their authority. Then dissensions among themselves, and the struggles of numerous claimants for the throne at Saraï broke the Golden-Horde into five Khanates each claiming supremacy.

CHAPTER IX.PASSING OF BYZANTIUM—MONGOL YOKE BROKEN

Something else had been taking place during these two centuries: something which involved the future, not alone of Russia, but of all Europe. In 1250, just ten years before Daniel established the line of Princes in Moscow, a little band of marauding Turks were encamped upon a plain in Asia Minor. They were led by an adventurer named Etrogruhl. For some service rendered to the ruler of the land Etrogruhl received a strip of territory as his reward, and when he died his son Othman displayed such ability in increasing his inheritance by absorbing the lands of other people that he became the terror of his neighbors. He had laid the foundation of the Ottoman empire and was the first of a line of thirty-five sovereigns, extending down to the present time. It is the descendant of Othman and of Etrogruhl the adventurer who sits to-day at Constantinople blocking the path to the East and defying Christendom. These Ottoman Turks were going to accomplish what Russian Princes from the time of Rurik and Oleg had longed and failed to do. They were going to break the power of the old empire in the East and make the coveted city on the Bosphorus their own. In 1453, the successor of Othman was in Constantinople.

The Pope, always hoping for a reconciliation, and always striving for the headship of a united Christendom, had in 1439 made fresh overtures to the Greek Church. The Emperor at Constantinople, three of the Patriarchs, and seventeen of the Metropolitans—including the one at Moscow—at last signed the Act of Union. But when the astonished Russians heard the prayer for the Pope, and saw the Latin cross upon their altars, their indignation knew no bounds. The Grand Prince Vasili so overwhelmed the Metropolitan with insults that he could not remain in Moscow, and the Union was abandoned. Its wisdom as a political measure cannot be doubted. If the Emperor had had the sympathy of the Pope, and the championship of Catholic Europe, the Turks might not have entered Constantinople in 1453. But they had not that sympathy, and the Turks did enter it; and no one event has ever left so lasting an impress upon civilization as the overthrow of the old Byzantine Empire, and the giving to the winds, to carry whither they would, its hoarded treasures of ancient ideals. Byzantium had been the heir to Greece, and now Russia claimed to be heir to Byzantium; while the head of Russia was Moscow, and the head of Moscow was Ivan III., who had just settled himself firmly on the seat left by his father, "Vasili the Blind" (1462).

Christendom had never received such a blow. Where had been before a rebellious and alienated brother, who might in time be reconciled, there was now—and at the very Gate of Europe—the infidel Turk, the bitterest and most dangerous foe to Christianity; bearing the same hated emblem that Charles Martel had driven back over the Pyrenees (in 732), and which had enslaved the

Spanish Peninsula for seven hundred years; but, unlike the Saracen, bringing barbarism instead of enlightenment in its train.

The Pope, in despair and grief, turned toward Russia. Its Metropolitan had become a Patriarch now, and the headship of the Greek Church had passed from Constantinople to Moscow. A niece of the last Greek Emperor, John Paleologus, had taken refuge in Rome; and when the Pope suggested the marriage of this Greek Princess Zoë with Ivan III., the proposition was joyfully accepted by him. After changing her name from Zoë to Sophia, and making a triumphal journey through Russia, this daughter of the Emperors reached Moscow and became the bride of Ivan III. Moscow had long been the ecclesiastical head of Russia; now she was the spiritual head of the Church in the East, and her ruling family was joined to that of the Caesars. Russia had certainly fallen heir to all that was left of the wreck of the Empire, and her future sovereigns might trace their lineage back to the Roman Caesars!

Moscow, by its natural position, was the distributing center of Russian products. The wood from the North, the corn from the fertile lands, and the food from the cattle region all poured into her lap, making her the commercial as well as the spiritual and political center. Now there flowed to that favored city another enriching stream. Following in the train of Ivan's Greek wife, were scholars, statesmen, diplomatists, artists. A host of Greek emigrants fleeing from the Turks, took refuge in Moscow, bringing with them books, manuscripts, and priceless treasures rescued from the ruined Empire. If this was a period of Renaissance for Western Europe, was it not rather a Naissance for Russia? What must have been the Russian people when her princes were still only barbarians? If Ivan valued these things, it was because they had been worn by Byzantium, and to him they symbolized power. There was plenty of rough work for him to do yet. There were Novgorod and her sister-republic Pskof to be wiped out, and Sweden and the Livonian Order on his borders to be looked after, Bulgaria and other lands to be absorbed, and last and most important of all, the Mongol yoke to be broken. And while he was planning for these he had little time for Greek manuscripts; he was introducing the knout,[1] until then a stranger to his Slavonic people; he was having Princes and boyars and even ecclesiastics whipped and tortured and mutilated; and, it is said, roasted alive two Polish gentlemen in an iron cage, for conspiracy. We hear that women fainted at his glance, and boyars trembled while he slept; that instead of "Ivan the Great" he would be known as "Ivan the Terrible," had not his grandson Ivan IV. so far outshone him. That he had his softer moods we know. For he loved his Greek wife, and shed tears copiously over his brother's death, even while he was appropriating all the territory which had belonged to him. And so great was his grief over the death of his only son, that he ordered the physicians who had attended him to be publicly beheaded!

The art of healing seems to have been a dangerous calling at that time. A learned German physician, named Anthony, in whom Ivan placed much confidence, was sent by him to attend a Tatar Prince who was a visitor at his court. When the Prince died after taking a decoction of herbs prepared by the physician, Ivan gave him up to the Tatar relatives of the deceased, to do with him as they liked. They took him down to the river Moskwa under the bridge, where they cut him in pieces like a sheep.

Ivan III. was not a warrior Prince like his great progenitors at Kief. It was even suspected that he lacked personal courage. He rarely led his armies to battle. His greatest triumphs were achieved sitting in his palace in the Kremlin; and his weapons were found in a cunning and far-reaching diplomacy. He swept away the system of appanages, and one by one effaced the privileges and the old legal and judicial systems in those Principalities which were not yet entirely absorbed. While maintaining an outward respect for Mongol authority, and while receiving its friendly aid in his attacks upon Novgorod and Lithuania, he was carefully laying his plans for open defiance. He cunningly refrained from paying tribute and homage on the pretense that he could not decide which of the five was lawful Khan.

In 1478 an embassy arrived at Moscow to collect tribute, bringing as the symbol of their authority an image of the Khan Akhmet. Ivan tore off the mask of friendship. In a fury he trampled the image under his feet and (it is said) put to death all except one whom he sent back with his message to the Golden Horde. The astonished Khan sent word that he would pardon him if he would come to Saraï and kiss his stirrup.

At last Ivan consented to lead his own army to meet that of the enraged Khan. The two armies confronted each other on the banks of the Oka. Then after a pause of several days, suddenly both were seized with a panic and fled. And so in this inglorious fashion in 1480, after three centuries of oppression and insult, Russia slipped from under the Mongol yoke. There were many Mongol invasions after this. Many times did they unite with Lithuanians and Poles and the enemies of Russia; many times were they at the gates of Moscow, and twice did they burn that city— excepting the Kremlin—to the ground. But never again was there homage or tribute paid to the broken and demoralized Asiatic power which long lingered about the Crimea. There are to-day two millions of nomad Mongols encamped about the south-eastern steppes of Russia, still living in tents, still raising and herding their flocks, little changed in dress, habits, and character since the days of Genghis Khan. While this is written a famine is said to be raging among them. This is the last remnant of the great Mongol invasion.

In 1487 Ivan marched upon Kazan. The city was taken after a siege of seven weeks. The Tsar of Kazan was a prisoner in Moscow and "Prince of Bulgaria" was added to the titles of Ivan III.

[1] From the word knot.

CHAPTER X.GRAND PRINCE BECOMES TSAR

Vasili, who succeeded Ivan III. in 1505, continued his work on the same lines of absorption and consolidation by unmerciful means. Pskof,—the sister republic to Novgorod the Great,—which had guarded its liberties with the same passionate devotion, was obliged to submit. The bell which had always summoned their Vetché, and which symbolized their liberty, was carried away. Their lament is as famous as that for the Moorish city of Alhama, when taken by Ferdinand of Aragon. The poetic annalist says: "Alas! glorious city of Pskof—why this weeping and lamentation?" Pskof replies: "How can I but weep and lament? An eagle with claws like a lion has swooped down upon me. He has captured my beauty, my riches, my children. Our land is a desert! our city ruined. Our brothers have been carried away to a place where our fathers never dwelt—nor our grandfathers—nor our great-grandfathers!" In the whole tragic story of Russia nothing is more pathetic and picturesque than the destruction of the two republics—Novgorod and Pskof.

By 1523 the last state had yielded, and the Muscovite absorption was complete. There was but one Russia; and the head of the consolidated empire called himself not "Grand Prince of all the Russias," but Tsar. When it is remembered that Tsar is only the Slavonic form for Caesar, it will be seen that the dream of the Varangian Princes had been in an unexpected way realized. The Tsar of Russia was the successor of the Caesars in the East.

Vasili's method of choosing a wife was like that of Ahasuerus. Fifteen hundred of the most beautiful maidens of noble birth were assembled at Moscow. After careful scrutiny the number was reduced to ten, then to five—from these the final choice was made. His wife's relations formed the court of Vasili, became his companions and advisers, boyars vying with each other for the privilege of waiting upon his table or assisting at his toilet. But the office of adviser was a difficult one. To one great lord who in his inexperience ventured to offer counsel, as in the olden time of the Drujina, he said sharply: "Be silent, rustic." While still another, more indiscreet, who had ventured to complain that they were not consulted, was ordered to his bedchamber, and there had his head cut off.

The court grew in barbaric and in Greek splendor. As the Tsar sat upon the throne supported by mechanical lions which roared at intervals, he was guarded by young nobles with high caps of white fur, wearing long caftans of white satin and armed with silver hatchets. Greek scholarship was also there. A learned monk and friend of Savonarola was translating Greek books and arranging for him the priceless volumes in his library. Vasili himself was now in correspondence with Pope Leo X., who was using all his arts to induce him to make friends with Catholic Poland and join in the most important of all wars—a war upon Constantinople, of which he, Vasili, the spiritual and temporal heir to the Eastern Empire, was the natural protector.

All this was very splendid. But things were moving with the momentum gained by his father,

Ivan the Great. It was Vasili's inheritance, not his reign, that was great. That inheritance he had maintained and increased. He had humiliated the nobility, had developed the movements initiated by his greater father, and had also shown tastes magnificent enough for the heir of his imperial mother, Sophia Paleologus. But he is overshadowed in history by standing between the two Ivans—Ivan the Great and Ivan the Terrible.

Leo X. was soon too much occupied with a new foe to think about designs upon Constantinople. A certain monk was nailing a protest upon the door of the Church at Wittenburg which would tax to the uttermost his energies. As from time to time travelers brought back tales of the splendor of the Muscovite court, Europe was more than ever afraid of such neighbors. What might these powerful barbarians not do, if they adopted European methods! More stringent measures were enforced. They must not have access to the implements of civilization, and Sigismund, King of Poland, threatened English merchants on the Baltic with death.

It is a singular circumstance that although, up to the time of Ivan the Great, Russia had apparently not one thing in common with the states of Western Europe, they were still subject to the same great tides or tendencies and were moving simultaneously toward identical political conditions. An invisible but compelling hand had been upon every European state, drawing the power from many heads into one. In Spain, Ferdinand and Isabella had brought all the smaller kingdoms and the Moors under one united crown. In France, Louis XI. had shattered the fabric of feudalism, and by artful alliance with the people had humiliated and subjugated the proud nobility. Henry VIII. had established absolutism in England, and Maximilian had done the same for Germany, while even the Italian republics, were being gathered into the hands of larger sovereignties. From this distance in time it is easy to see the prevailing direction in which all the nations were being irresistibly drawn.

The hour had struck for the tide to flow toward centralisation; and Russia, remote, cut off from all apparent connection with the Western kingdoms, was borne along upon the same tide with the rest, as if it was already a part of the same organism! There, too, the power was passing from the many to one: first from many ruling families to one family, then from all the individual members of that family to a supreme and permanent head—the Tsar.

There were many revolutions in Russia from the time when the Dolgorukis turned the life-currents from Kief to the North; many centers of volcanic energy in fearful state of activity, and many times when ruin threatened from every side. But in the midst of all this there was one steady process—one end being always approached—a consolidation and a centralization of authority before which European monarchies would pale! The process commenced with the autocratic purposes of Andrew Bogoliubski. And it was because his boyars instinctively knew that the success of his policy meant their ruin that they assassinated him.

In "Old Russia" a close and fraternal tie bound the Prince and his Drujina together. It was one family, of which he was the adored head. What characterized the "New Russia" was a growing antagonism between the Grand Prince and his lords or boyars. This developed into a life-and-death struggle, similar to that between Louis XI. and his nobility. His elevation meant their humiliation. It was a terrible clash of forces—a duel in which one was the instrument of fate, and the other predestined to destruction.

It was of less importance during the period between Andrew Bogoliubski and Ivan IV. that Mongols were exercising degrading tyranny and making desperate reprisals for defeat—that Lithuania and Poland, and conspirators everywhere, were by arms and by diplomacy and by treachery trying to ruin the state; all this was of less import than the fact that every vestige of authority was surely passing out of the hands of the nobility into those of the Tsar. The fight was a desperate one. It became open and avowed under Ivan III., still more bitter under his son Vasili II., and culminated at last under Ivan the Terrible, when, like an infuriated animal, he let loose upon them all the pent-up instincts in his blood.

CHAPTER XI.IVAN THE TERRIBLE— ACQUISITION OF SIBERIA

In 1533 Vasili II. died, leaving the scepter to Ivan IV., an infant son three years old. Now the humiliated Princes and boyars were to have their turn. The mother of Ivan IV., Helena Glinski, was the only obstacle in their way. She speedily died, the victim of poison, and then there was no one to stem the tide of princely and oligarchic reaction against autocracy; and the many years of Ivan's minority would give plenty of time to re-establish their lost authority. The boyars took possession of the government. Ivan wrote later: "My brother and I were treated like the children of beggars. We were half clothed, cold, and hungry." The boyars in the presence of these children appropriated the luxuries and treasures in the palace and then plundered the people as well, exacting unmerciful fines and treating them like slaves. The only person who loved the neglected Ivan was his nurse, and she was torn from him; and for a courtier to pity the forlorn child was sufficient for his downfall. Ivan had a superior intelligence. He read much and was keenly observant of all that was happening. He saw himself treated with insolent contempt in private, but with abject servility in public. He also observed that his signature was required to give force to everything that was done, and so discovered that he was the rightful master, that the real power was vested only in him. Suddenly, in 1543, he sternly summoned his court to come into his presence, and, ordering the guards to seize the chief offender among his boyars, he then and there had him torn to pieces by his hounds. This was a coup d'état by a boy of thirteen! He was content with the banishment of many others, and then Ivan IV. peacefully commenced his reign. He seemed a gentle, indolent youth; very confiding in those he trusted; inclined to be a voluptuary, loving pleasure and study and everything better than affairs of state. In 1547 he was crowned Tsar of Russia, and soon thereafter married Anastasia of the house of Romanoff, whom he devotedly loved. As was the custom, he surrounded himself with his mother's and his wife's relations. So the Glinskis and the Romanoffs were the envied families in control of the government. His mother's family, the Glinskis, were especially unpopular; and when a terrific fire destroyed nearly the whole of Moscow it was whispered by jealous boyars that the Princess Anna Glinski had brought this misfortune upon them by enchantments. She had taken human hearts, boiled them in water, and then sprinkled the houses where the fire started! An enraged populace burst into the palace of the Glinskis, murdering all they could find.

Ivan, nervous and impressionable, seems to have been profoundly affected by all this. He yielded to the popular demand and appointed two men to administer the government, spiritual and temporal—Adashef, belonging to the smaller nobility, and Silvester, a priest. Believing absolutely in their fidelity, he then concerned himself very little about affairs of state, and engaged in the completion of the work commenced by Ivan III.—a revision of the old code of laws established by Yaroslaf. These were very peaceful and very happy years for Russia and for himself. But Ivan was stricken with a fever, and while apparently in a dying condition he discovered the treachery of his trusted ministers, that they were shamefully intriguing with his Tatar enemies. When he heard their rejoicings that the day of the Glinskis and the Romanoffs was over, he realized the fate awaiting Anastasia and her infant son if he died. He resolved that he would not die.

Banishment seems a light punishment to have inflicted. It was gentle treatment for treason at the court of Moscow. But the poison of suspicion had entered his soul, and was the more surely, because slowly, working a transformation in his character. And when soon thereafter Anastasia mysteriously and suddenly died, his whole nature seemed to be undergoing a change. He was passing from Ivan the gentle and confiding, into "Ivan the Terrible."

Ivan said later, in his own vindication: "When that dog Adashef betrayed me, was anyone put to death? Did I not show mercy? They say now that I am cruel and irascible; but to whom? I am cruel toward those that are cruel to me. The good! ah, I would give them the robe and the chain that I wear! My subjects would have given me over to the Tatars, sold me to my enemies. Think of the enormity of the treason! If some were chastised, was it not for their crimes, and are they not my slaves—and shall I not do what I will with mine own?"

His grievances were real. His boyars were desperate and determined, and even with their foreheads in the dust were conspiring against him. They were no less terrible than he toward their inferiors. There never could be anything but anarchy in Russia so long as this aristocracy of cruel slave-masters existed. Ivan (like Louis XI.) was girding himself for the destruction of the power of his nobility, and, as one conspiracy after another was revealed, faster and faster flowed the torrent of his rage.

In 1571 he devoutly asked the prayers of the Church for 3470 of his victims, 986 of whom he mentioned by name; many of these being followed by the sinister addition: "With his wife and children"; "with his sons"; "with his daughters." A gentle, kindly Prince had been converted into a monster of cruelty, who is called, by the historians of his own country, the Nero of Russia.

He was a pious Prince, like all of the Muscovite line. Not one of his subjects was more faithful in religious observances than was this "torch of orthodoxy"—who frequently called up his household in the middle of the night for prayers. Added to the above pious petition for mercy to his victims, is this reference to Novgorod: "Remember, Lord, the souls of thy servants to the number of 1505 persons—Novgorodians, whose names, Almighty, thou knowest."

That Republic had made its last break for liberty. Under the leadership of Marfa, the widow of a wealthy and powerful noble, it had thrown itself in despair into the arms of Catholic Poland. This was treason to the Tsar and to the Church, and its punishment was awful. The desperate woman who had instigated the act was carried in chains to Moscow, there to behold her two sons with the rest of the conspirators beheaded. The bell which for centuries had summoned her citizens to the Vetché, that sacred symbol of the liberty of the Republic, is now in the Museum at Moscow. If its tongue should speak, if its clarion call should ring out once more, perhaps there might come from the shades a countless host of her martyred dead—"Whose names, Almighty, thou knowest." Ivan then proceeded to wreck the prosperity of the richest commercial city in his empire. Its trade was enormous with the East and the West. It had joined the Hanseatic League, and its wealth was largely due to the German merchants who had flocked there. With singular lack of wisdom, the Tsar had confiscated the property of these men, and now the ruin of the city was complete.

While Germany, and Poland, and Sweden,—resolved to shut up Russia in her barbaric isolation,—were locking the front door on the Baltic and the Gulf, England had found a side door by which to enter. With great satisfaction Ivan saw English traders coming in by way of the White Sea, and he extended the rough hand of his friendship to Queen Elizabeth, who made with him a commercial treaty, which was countersigned by Francis Bacon. Then, as his friendship warmed, he proposed that they should sign a reciprocal engagement to furnish each other with an asylum in the event of the rebellion of their subjects. Elizabeth declined the asylum he kindly offered her, "finding, by the grace of God, no dangers of the sort in her kingdom." Then he did her the honor to offer an alliance of a different kind. He proposed that she should send him her cousin Lady Mary Hastings to take the place left vacant by his eighth wife—to become his Tsaritsa. The proposition was considered, but when the English maiden heard about his brutalities and about his seven wives, so terrified was she that she refused to leave England, and the affair had to be abandoned. Elizabeth's rejection of his proposals, and also of his plan for an alliance offensive and defensive against Poland and Sweden, so infuriated Ivan that he confiscated the goods of the English merchants, and this friendship was temporarily ruptured. But amicable relations were soon restored between Elizabeth and her barbarian admirer. If she had heard of his awful vengeance in 1571, she had also heard of the massacre of St. Bartholomew in Paris in 1572!

Russia had now opened diplomatic relations with the Western kingdoms. The foreign ambassadors were received with great pomp in a sumptuous hall hung with tapestries and blazing with gold and silver. The Tsar, with crown and scepter, sat upon his throne, supported by the roaring lions, and carefully studied the new ambassador as he suavely asked him about his master. A police inspector from that moment never lost sight of him, making sure that he obtained no interviews with the natives nor information about the state of the country. Although the Tsar was reputed to be learned and was probably the most learned man in his nation, and had always about him a coterie of distinguished scholars, still there was no intellectual life in Russia, and owing to the Oriental seclusion of the women there was no society. The men were heavily bearded, and the ideal of beauty with the women, as they looked furtively out from behind veils and curtains, was to be fat, with red, white, and black paint laid on like a mask. It must have been a dreary post for gay European diplomats, and in marked contrast to gay, witty, gallant Poland, at that time thoroughly Europeanized.

Next to the consolidation of the imperial authority, the event in this reign most affecting the future of Russia was the acquisition of Siberia. A Cossack brigand under sentence of death escaped with his followers into the land beyond the Urals, and conquered a part of the territory, then returned and offered it to Ivan (1580) in exchange for a pardon. The incident is the subject of a bilina, a form of historical poem, in which Yermak says:

"I am the robber Hetman of the Don.

And now—oh—orthodox Tsar,
I bring you my traitorous head,
And with it I bring the Empire of Siberia!
And the orthodox Tsar will speak—
He will speak—the terrible Ivan,
Ha! thou art Yermak, the Hetman of the Don,
I pardon thee and thy band,
I pardon thee for thy trusty service—
And I give to the Cossack the glorious and gentle Don as an inheritance."

The two Ivans had created a new code of laws, and now there was an ample prison-house for its transgressors! The penal code was frightful. An insolvent debtor was tied up half naked in a public place and beaten three hours a day for thirty or forty days, and then, if no one came to his rescue, with his wife and his children he was sold as a slave. But Siberia was to be the prison-house of a more serious class of offenders for whom this punishment would be insufficient. It was to serve as a vast penal colony for crimes against the state. Since the beginning of the nineteenth century it is said one million political exiles have been sent there, and they continue to go at the rate of twenty thousand a year; showing how useful a present was made by the robber Yermak to the "Orthodox Tsar"!

This reign, like that of Louis XI. of France, which it much resembled, enlarged the privileges of the people in order to aid Ivan in his conflict with his nobility. For this purpose a Sobor, or States-General, was summoned by him, and met at long intervals thereafter until the time of Peter the First.

Of the two sons left to Ivan by his wife Anastasia, only one now remained. In a paroxysm of rage he had struck the Tsarevitch with his iron staff. He did not intend to kill him, but the blow was mortal. Great and fierce was the sorrow of the Tsar when he found he had slain his beloved son—the one thing he loved upon earth, and there remained to inherit the fruit of his labors and his crimes only another child (Feodor) enfeebled in body and mind, and an infant (Dmitri), the son of his seventh wife. His death, hastened by grief, took place three years later, in 1584.

CHAPTER XII.SERFDOM CREATED—THE FIRST ROMANOFF

Occasionally there arises a man in history who, without distinction of birth or other advantages, is strong enough by sheer ability to grasp the opportunity, vault into power, and then stem the tide of events. Such a man was Godwin, father of Harold, last Saxon King; in England; and such a man was Boris Godunof, a boyar, who had so faithfully served the terrible Ivan that he leaned upon him and at last confided to him the supervision of his feeble son Feodor, when he should succeed him. The plans of this ambitious usurper were probably laid from the time of the tragic death of Ivan's son, the Tsarevitch. He brought about the marriage of his beautiful sister Irene with Feodor, and from the hour of Ivan's death was virtual ruler. Dmitri, the infant son of the late Tsar, aged five years, was prudently placed at a distance—and soon thereafter mysteriously died (1591). There can be no doubt that the unexplained tragedy of this child's death was perfectly understood by Boris; and when Feodor also died, seven years later (1598), there was not one of the old Muscovite line to succeed to the throne. But so wise had been the administration of affairs by the astute Regent that a change was dreaded. A council offered him the crown, which he feigned a reluctance to accept, preferring that the invitation should come from a source which would admit of no question as to his rights in the future. Accordingly, the States-General or Sobor was convened, and Boris Godunof was chosen by acclamation.

The work of three reigns was undone. A boyar was Tsar of Russia—and a boyar not in the line of Rurik and with Tatar blood in his veins! But this bold and unscrupulous man had performed a service to the state. The work of the Muscovite Princes was finished, and the extinction of the line was the next necessary event in the path of progress.

Boris had large and comprehensive views and proceeded upon new lines of policy to reconstruct the state. He saw that Russia must be Europeanized, and he also saw that at least one radical change in her internal policy might be used to insure his popularity with the Princes and nobles. The Russian peasantry was an enormous force which was not utilized to its fullest extent. It included almost the entire rural population of Russia. The peasant was legally a freeman. He lived unchanged under the old Slavonic patriarchal system of Mirs, or communes, and Volosts. These were the largest political organizations of which he had personal cognizance. He knew nothing about Muscovite consolidation, nor oligarchy, nor autocracy. No crumbs from the modern banquet had fallen into his lap. With a thin veneer of orthodoxy over their paganism and superstition the people listened in childish wonder to the same old tales—they lived their old primitive life of toil under the same system of simple fair-dealing and justice. If their commune owned the land it tilled, they all shared the benefit of the harvests, paid their tax to the state, and all was well. If not, it swarmed like a community of bees to some wealthy neighbor's estate and sold its labor to him, and then if he proved too hard a taskmaster—even for a patient Russian peasant—they might swarm again and work for another.

The tie binding them to special localities was only the very slightest. There were no mountains to love, one part of the monotonous plateau was about like another; and as for their homes, their wooden huts were burned down so often there were no memories attached to them.

The result of this was that the peasantry—that immense force upon which the state at last depended—was not stable and permanent, but fluid. At the slightest invitation of better wages, or better soil or conditions, whole communities might desert a locality—would gather up their goods and walk off. Boris, while Regent, conceived the idea of correcting this evil, in a way which would at the same time make him a very popular ruler with the class whose support he most needed, the Princes and the landowners. He would chain the peasant to the soil. A decree was issued that henceforth the peasant must not go from one estate to another. He belonged to the land he was tilling, as the trees that grew on it belonged to it, and the master of that land was his master for evermore!

Such, in brief outline, was the system of serfdom which prevailed until 1861. It was in theory, though not practically, unlike the institution of American slavery. The people, still living in their communes, still clung to the figment of their freedom, not really understanding that they were slaves, but feeling rather that they were freemen whose sacred rights had been cruelly invaded. That they were giving to hard masters the fruit of their toil on their own lands.

Now that Russia was becoming a modern state, it required more money to govern her. Civilization is costly, and the revenues must not be fluctuating. Boris saw they could only be made sure by attaching to the soil the peasant, whose labor was at the foundation of the prosperity of the state. It was the peasant who bore the weight of an expanded civilization which he did not share! The visitor at Moscow to-day may see in the Kremlin a wonderful tower, 270 feet high, which was erected in honor of Ivan the Great by the usurper Boris; but the monument which keeps his memory alive is the more stupendous one of—Serfdom.

The expected increase in prosperity from the new system did not immediately come. The revenues were less than before. Bands of fugitive serfs were fleeing from their masters and joining the community of free Cossacks on the Don. Lands were untilled, there was misery, and at last there was famine, and then discontent and demoralization extending to the upper classes, and a diminished income which finally bore upon the Tsar himself.

Suddenly there came a rumor that Dmitri, the infant son of Ivan the Terrible, was not dead! He was living in Poland, and with incontestable proofs of his identity was coming to claim his own. In 1604 he crossed the frontier, and thousands of discontented people flocked to his standard with wild enthusiasm. Boris had died just before Dmitri reached Moscow. He entered the city, and the infatuated people placed in his hand and upon his head the scepter and the crown of Ivan IV.; and after making sure that the wife and the son of Boris Godunof were strangled, this amazing Pretender commenced his reign.

An extraordinary thing had happened. A nameless adventurer and impostor had been received with tears of joy as the son of Ivan and of St. Vladimir, the seventh wife of Ivan the Terrible even recognizing and embracing him as her son! But Dmitri had not the wisdom to keep what his cunning had won. His Polish wife came, followed by a suite of Polish Catholics, who began to carry things with a high hand. The clergy was offended and soon enraged. In five years Dmitri was assassinated, and his mutilated corpse was lying in the palace at the Kremlin, an object of insult and derision; and then, for Russia there came another chaos.

For a brief period Vasili Shuiski, head of one of the princely families, reigned, while two more "false Dmitris" appeared, one from Sweden and the other from Poland. The cause of the latter was upheld by the King of Poland, with the ulterior purpose of bringing the disordered state of Russia under the Polish crown, and making one great Slav kingdom with its center at Cracow.

So disorganized had the State become that some of the Princes had actually opened negotiations with Sigismund with a view to offering the crown to his son. But when Sigismund with an invading army was in Moscow (1610), and when Vasili Shuiski was a prisoner in Poland, and a Polish Prince was claiming the title of Tsar, there came an awakening—not among the nobility, but deep down in the heart of orthodox Russia. From this awakening of a dormant national sentiment and of the religious instincts of the people there developed that event,—the most health-restoring which can come to the life of a nation,—a national uprising in which all classes unite in averting a common disaster. What disaster could be for Russia more terrible than an absorption into Catholic Poland? The Polish intruders and pretenders were driven out, and then a great National Assembly gathered at Moscow (1613) to elect a Tsar.

The name of Romanoff was unstained by crime, and was by maternal ancestry allied to the royal race of Rurik. The newly awakened patriotism turned instinctively toward that, as the highest expression of their hopes; and Mikhail Romanoff, a youth of 16, was elected Tsar.

It was in 1547 that Anastasia, of the House of Romanoff, had married Ivan IV. At about the same time her brother was married to a Princess of Suzdal, a descendant of the brother of Alexander Nevski. This Princess was the grandmother of Mikhail Romanoff, and the source from which has sprung the present ruling house in Russia.

CHAPTER XIII. NIKON'S ATTEMPT— RASKOLNIKS

In the building of an empire there are two processes—the building up, and the tearing down. The plow is no less essential than the trowel. The period after Boris had been for Russia the period of the wholesome plow. The harvest was far off. But the name Romanoff was going to stand for another Russia, not like the old Russia of Kief, nor yet the new Russia of Moscow; but another and a Europeanized Russia, in which, after long struggles, the Slavonic and half-Asiatic giant was going to tear down the walls of separation, escape from his barbarism, and compel Europe to share with him her civilization.

The man who was to make the first breach in the walls was the grandson of Mikhail Romanoff—Peter, known as "The Great." But the mills of the gods grind slowly—especially when they have a great work in hand; and there were to be three colorless reigns before the coming of the Liberator in 1689—seventy-six years before they would learn that to have a savage despot seated on a barbaric throne, with crown and robes incrusted with jewels, and terrorizing a brutish, ignorant, and barbaric people—was not to be Great.

The reigns of Mikhail and of his son Alexis and his grandson Feodor were to be reigns of preparation and reform. Of course there were turbulent uprisings and foreign wars, and perils on the frontiers near the Baltic and the Black seas. But Russia was gaining in ascendency while Poland, from whom she had narrowly escaped, was fast declining. The European rulers began to see advantages for themselves from Russian alliances. Gustavus Adolphus, King of Sweden and champion of Protestantism, made an eloquent appeal to the Tsar to join him against Catholic Poland—"Was not the Romish Church their common enemy?—and were they not neighbors?—and when your neighbor's house is afire, is it not the part of wisdom and prudence to help to put it out?" Poland suffered a serious blow when a large body of Cossacks, who were her vassals, and her chief arm of defense in the Southeast, in 1681 transferred themselves bodily to Russia.

The Cossacks were a Slavonic people, with no doubt a plentiful infusion of Asiatic blood, and their name in the Tatar language meant Freebooters. They had long dwelt about the Don and the Dnieper, in what is known as Little Russia, a free and rugged community which was recruited by Russians after the Tatar invasion and Polish conquest, by oppressed peasants after the creation of serfdom, and by adventurers and fugitives from justice at all times. It was a military organization, and its Constitution was a pure democracy. Freedom and independence were their first necessity. Their Hetman, or chief, held office for one year only, and anyone might attain to that position. Their horsemanship was unrivaled—they were fearless and enduring, and stood ready to sell their services to the Khan of Tatary, the King of Poland, or to the Tsar of Russia. In fact, they were the Northmen of the South and East, and are now—the Rough-Riders of Russia.

They had long ago divided into two bands, the "Cossacks of the Dnieper," loosely bound to Poland, and the "Cossacks of the Don," owning the sovereignty of Russia. The services of these fearless adventurers were invaluable as a protection from Turks and Tatars; and, as we have seen in the matter of Siberia, they sometimes brought back prizes which offset their misdoings. The King of Poland unwisely attempted to proselyte his Cossacks of the Dnieper, sent Jesuit missionaries among them, and then concluded to break their spirit by severities and make of them obedient loyal Catholic subjects. He might as well have tried to chain the winds. They offered to the Tsar their allegiance in return for his protection, and in 1681 all of the Cossacks, of the Dnieper as well as the Don, were gathered under Russian sovereignty. It was this event which, in the long struggle with Poland, turned the scales at last in favor of Russia.

One of the most important occurrences in this reign was the attempt of the Patriarch Nikon to establish an authority in the East similar to that of the Pope in the West—and in many ways to Latinize the Church. This attempt to place the Tsar under spiritual authority was put down by a popular revolt—followed by stricter orthodox methods in a sect known as the Raskolniks.

Mikhail died in 1645, and was succeeded by his son Alexis. The new Tsar sent an envoy to Charles the First of England to announce his succession. He arrived with his letter to the King at an inopportune time. He was on trial for his life. The Russian could not comprehend such a condition, and haughtily refused to treat with anyone but the King. He was received with much ceremony by the House of Lords, and then to their consternation arose and said: "I have come from my sovereign charged with an important message to your King—Charles the First. It is long since I came, and I have not been permitted to see him nor to deliver the letter from my master." The embarrassed English boyars replied that they would give their reasons for this by letter. When the Tsar was informed by Charles II. of the execution of his father, sternly inflicted by his people, he could not comprehend such a condition. He at once forbade English merchants to live in any of his cities except Archangel, and sent money and presents to the exiled son.

An interest attaches to the marriage of Alexis with Natalia, his second wife. He was dining with one of his boyars and was attracted by a young girl, who was serving him. She was motherless, and had been adopted by her uncle the boyar. The Tsar said to his friend soon after: "I have found a husband for your Natalia." The husband was Alexis himself, and Natalia became the mother of Peter the Great. She was the first Princess who ever drew aside the curtains of her litter and permitted the people to look upon her face. Thrown much into the society of Europeans in her uncle's home, she was imbued with European ideas. It was no doubt she who first instilled the leaven of reform into the mind of her infant son Peter.

One of the most important features of this reign was the development of the fanatical sect known as Raskolniks. They are the dissenters or non-conformists of Russia. Their existence dates from the time of the Patriarch Nikon—and what they considered his sacrilegious innovations. But as early as 1476 there were the first stirrings of this movement when some daring and advanced innovators began to sing "O Lord, have mercy," instead of "Lord, have Mercy," and to say "Alleluia" twice instead of three times, to the peril of their souls! But it was in the reign of Alexis that signs of falling away from the faith spoken of in the Apocalypse were unmistakable. Foreign heretics who shaved their chins and smoked the accursed weed were tolerated in Holy Moscow. "The number of the Beast" indicated the year 1666. It was evident that the end of the world was at hand! Such was the beginning of the Raskolniks, who now number 10,000,000 souls—a conservative Slavonic element which has been a difficult one to deal with.

Upon the death of Alexis, in 1676, his eldest son Feodor succeeded him. It is only necessary to mention one significant act in his short reign—the destruction of the Books of Pedigrees. The question of precedence among the great families was the source of endless disputes, and no man would accept a position inferior to any held by his ancestors, nor would serve under a man with an ancestry inferior to his own. Feodor asked that the Books of Pedigrees be sent to him for examination, and then had them every one thrown into the fire and burned. This must have been his last act, for his death and this holocaust of ancestral claims both occurred in the year 1682.

CHAPTER XIV. PETER STUDIES EUROPEAN CIVILIZATION

A history of Russia naïvely designates one of its chapters "The Period of Troubles"! When was there not a period of troubles in this land? The historian wearies, and doubtless the reader too, of such prolonged disorder and calamity. But a chapter telling of peace and tranquillity would have to be invented. The particular sort of trouble that developed upon the death of Feodor was of a new variety. Alexis had left two families of children, one by his first wife and the other by Natalia. There is not time to tell of all the steps by which Sophia, daughter of the first marriage, came to be the power behind the throne upon which sat her feeble brother Ivan, and her half-brother Peter, aged ten years. Sophia was an ambitious, strong-willed, strong-minded woman, who dared to emancipate herself from the tyranny of Russian custom.

The terem, of which we hear so much, was the part of the palace sacred to the Tsaritsa and the Princesses—upon whose faces no man ever looked. If a physician were needed he might feel the pulse and the temperature through a piece of gauze—but see the face never. It is said that two nobles who one day accidentally met Natalia coming from her chapel were deprived of rank in consequence.

But the terem, with "its twenty-seven locks," was not going to confine the sister of Peter. She met the eyes of men in public; studied them well, too; and then selected the instruments for her designs of effacing Peter and his mother, and herself becoming sovereign indeed. A rumor was circulated that the imbecile Ivan (who was alive) had been strangled by Natalia's family. In the tumult which followed one of her brothers, Peter's uncle, was torn from Natalia's arms and cut to pieces. But this was only one small incident in the horrid tragedy. Then, after discovering that the Prince was not dead, the bloodstains in the palace were washed up, and the two brothers were placed upon the throne under the Regency of Sophia. But while she was outraging the feelings of the people by her contempt for ancient customs, and while her friendship with her Minister, Prince Galitsuin, was becoming a public scandal, Sophia was at the same time being defeated in a campaign against the Turks at the Crimea; and her popularity was gone.

In the meantime Peter was growing. With no training, no education, he was in his own disorderly, undisciplined fashion struggling up into manhood under the tutelage of a quick, strong intelligence, a hungry desire to know, and a hot, imperious temper. His first toys were drums and swords, and he first studied history from colored German prints; and as he grew older never wearied of reading about Ivan the Terrible. His delight was to go out upon the streets of Moscow and pick up strange bits of information from foreign adventurers about the habits and customs of their countries. He played at soldiers with his boy companions, and after finding how they did such things in Germany and in England, drilled his troops after the European fashion. But it was when he first saw a boat so built that it could go with or against the wind, that his strongest instinct was awakened. He would not rest until he had learned how to make and then to manage it. When this strange, passionate, self-willed boy was seventeen years old, he realized that his sister was scheming for the ruin of himself and his mother. In the rupture that followed, the people deserted Sophia and flocked about Peter. He placed his sister in a monastery, where, after fifteen years of fruitless intrigue and conspiracy, she was to die. Then, conjointly with his unfortunate brother, he commenced his reign (1689).

If Sophia had freed herself from the customary seclusion of Princesses, Peter emancipated himself from the usual proprieties of the palace. Both were scandalous. One had harangued soldiers and walked with her veil lifted, the other was swinging an ax like a carpenter, rowing like a Cossack, or fighting mimic battles with his grooms, who not infrequently knocked him down. In 1693 he gratified one great thirst and longing. With a large suite he went up to Archangel—and for the first time a Tsar looked out upon the sea! He ate and drank with the foreign merchants, and took deep draughts of the stimulating air from the west. He established a dock-yard, and while his first ship was building made perilous trips upon that unknown ocean from which Russia had all its life been shut out! His ship was the first to bear a Russian flag into foreign waters, and now Peter had taken the first step toward learning how to build a navy, but he had no place yet to use one. So he turned his nimble activities toward the Black Sea. He had only to capture Azof in the Crimea from the Turks, and he would have a sea for his navy—and then might easily make the navy for his sea! So he went down, carrying his soldiers and his new European tactics—in which no one believed—gathered up his Cossacks, and the attack was made, first with utter failure—all on account of the new tactics—and then at last came overwhelming success; and a triumphant return (1676) to Moscow under arches and garlands of flowers. Three thousand Russian families were sent to colonize Azof, which was guarded by some regiments of the Streltsui and by Cossacks—and now there must be a navy.

There must be nine ships of the line, and twenty frigates carrying fifty guns, and bombships, and fireships. That would require a great deal of money. It was then that the utility of the system of serfdom became apparent. The prelates and monasteries were taxed—one vessel to every eighty thousand serfs!—according to their wealth all the orders of nobility to bear their portion in the same way, and the peasants toiled on, never dreaming that they were building a great navy for the great Tsar. Peter then sent fifty young nobles of the court to Venice, England, and the Netherlands to learn the arts of shipbuilding and seamanship and gunnery. But how could he be sure of the knowledge and the science of these idle youths—unless he himself owned it and knew better than they? The time had come for his long-indulged dream of visiting the Western kingdoms.

But while there were rejoicings at the victory over the Turks, there was a feeling of universal disgust at the new order of things; with the militia (the Streltsui) because foreigners were preferred to them and because they were subjected to an unaccustomed discipline; with the nobles because their children were sent into foreign lands among heretics to learn trades like mechanics; and with the landowners and clergy because the cost of equipping a great fleet fell upon them. All classes were ripe for a revolt.

Sophia, from her cloister, was in correspondence with her agents, and a conspiracy ripened to overthrow Peter and his reforms. As the Tsar was one evening sitting down to an entertainment with a large party of ladies and gentlemen, word was brought that someone desired to see him privately upon an important matter. He promptly excused himself and was taken in a sledge to the appointed place. There he graciously sat down to supper with a number of gentlemen, as if perfectly ignorant of their plans. Suddenly his guard arrived, entered the house, and arrested the entire party, after which Peter returned in the best of humor to his interrupted banquet, quite as if nothing had happened. The next day the prisoners under torture revealed the plot to assassinate him and then lay it to the foreigners, this to be followed, by a general massacre of Europeans— men, women, and children. The ringleaders were first dismembered, then beheaded—their legs and arms being displayed in conspicuous places in the city, and the rest of the conspirators, excepting his sister Sophia, were sent to Siberia.

With this parting and salutary lesson to his subjects in 1697, Peter started upon his strange travels—in quest of the arts of civilization!

The embassy was composed of 270 persons. Among them was a young man twenty-five years old, calling himself Peter Mikhailof, who a few weeks later might have been seen at Saardam in Holland, in complete outfit of workman's clothes, in dust and by the sweat of his brow learning the art of ship-carpentry. Such was the first introduction to Europe of the Tsar of Russia! They had long heard of this autocrat before whom millions trembled, ruling like a savage despot in the midst of splendors rivaling the Arabian Nights. Now they saw him! And the amazement can scarcely be described. He dined with the Great Electress Sophia, afterwards first Queen of Prussia, and she wrote of him: "Nature has given him an infinity of wit. With advantages he might have been an accomplished man. What a pity his manners are not less boorish!"

But Peter was not thinking of the impression he made. With an insatiable inquisitiveness and an omnivorous curiosity, he was looking for the secret of power in nations. Nothing escaped him—cutlery, rope-making, paper manufacture, whaling industry, surgery, microscopy; he was engaging artists, officers, engineers, surgeons, buying models of everything he saw—or standing lost in admiration of a traveling dentist plying his craft in the market, whom he took home to his lodgings, learned the use of the instruments himself, then practiced his new art upon his followers.

At The Hague he endured the splendid public reception, then hurried off his gold-trimmed coat, his wig and hat and white feathers, and was amid grime and dust examining grist-mills, and ferry-boats, and irrigating machines. To a lady he saw on the street at Amsterdam he shouted "Stop!" then dragged out her enameled watch, examined it, and put it back without a word. A nobleman's wig in similar unceremonious fashion he snatched from his head, turned it inside out, and, not being pleased with its make, threw it on the floor.

Perhaps Holland heard without regret that her guest was going to England, where he was told the instruction was based upon the principles of ship-building and he might learn more in a few weeks than by a year's study elsewhere. King William III. placed a fleet at his disposal, and also a palace upon his arrival in London. A violent storm alarmed many on the way to England, but Peter enjoyed it and humorously said, "Did you ever hear of a Tsar being lost in the North Sea?"

England was no less astonished than Holland at her guest, but William III., the wisest sovereign in Europe, we learn was amazed at the vigor and originality of his mind. The wise Bishop Burnet wrote of him: "He is mechanically turned, and more fitted to be a carpenter than a Prince. He told me he designed a great fleet for attacking the Turkish Empire, but he does not seem to me capable of so great an enterprise." This throws more light upon the limitations of Bishop Burnet than those of Peter the Great, and fairly illustrates the incompetency of contemporary estimates of genius; or, perhaps, the inability of talent to take the full measure of genius at any time. The good Bishop adds that he adores the wise Providence which "has raised up such a furious man to reign over such a part of the world." Louis XIV. "had procured the postponement of the honor of his visit"; so Peter prepared, after visiting Vienna, to go to Venice, but receiving disturbing news of matters at home, this uncivilized civilizer, this barbarian reformer of barbarism, turned his face toward Moscow.

There was widespread dissatisfaction in the empire. The Streltsui (militia) was rebellious, the heavily taxed landowners were angry, and the people disgusted by the prevalence of German clothes and shaved faces. Had not the wise Ivan IV. said: "To shave is a sin that the blood of all the martyrs could not cleanse"! And who had ever before seen a Tsar of Moscow quit Holy Russia to wander in foreign lands among Turks and Germans? for both were alike to them. Then it was rumored that Peter had gone in disguise to Stockholm, and that the Queen of Sweden had put him into a cask lined with nails to throw him into the sea, and he had only been saved by one of his guards taking his place; and some years later many still believed that it was a false Tsar who returned to them in 1700—that the true Tsar was still a prisoner at Stockholm, attached to a post. Sophia wrote to the Streltsui—"You suffer—but you will suffer more. Why do you wait? March on Moscow. There is no news of the Tsar." The army was told that he was dead, and that the boyars were scheming to kill his infant son Alexis and then get into power again. Thousands of revolted troops from Azof began to pour into Moscow, then there was a rumor that the foreigners and the Germans—who were introducing the smoking of tobacco and shaving, to the utter destruction of the holy faith—were planning to seize the town. Peter returned to find Moscow the prey to wild disorder, in the hands of scheming revolutionists and mutineers. He concluded it was the right time to give a lesson which would never be forgotten. He would make the partisans of Old Russia feel the weight of his hand in a way that would remind them of Ivan IV.

On the day of his return the nobles all presented themselves, laying their faces, as was the custom, in the dust. After courteously returning their salutations, Peter ordered that every one of them be immediately shaved; and as this was one of the arts he had practiced while abroad he initiated the process by skillfully applying the razor himself to a few of the long-beards. Then the inquiry into the rebellion commenced. The Patriarch tried to appease the wrath of the Tsar, who answered; "Know that I venerate God and his Mother as much as you do. But also know that I shall protect my people and punish rebels." The "chastisement" was worthy of Ivan the Terrible. The details of its infliction are too dreadful to relate, and we read with incredulous horror that "the terrible carpenter of Saardam plied his own ax in the horrible employment"—and that on the last day Peter himself put to death eighty-four of the Streltsui, "compelling his boyars to assist"—in inflicting this "chastisement!"

CHAPTER XV.CHARLES XII.—NARVA—ST. PETERSBURG

The Baltic was at this time a Swedish sea. Finland, Livonia, and all the territory on the eastern coast, where once the Russians and the German knights had struggled, was now under the sovereignty of an inexperienced young king who had just ascended the throne of his father Charles XI., King of Sweden. If Peter ever "opened a window" into the West, it must be done by first breaking through this Swedish wall. Livonia was deeply aggrieved just now because of some oppressive measures against her, and her astute minister, Patkul, suggested to the King of Poland that he form a coalition between that kingdom, Denmark, and Russia for the purpose of breaking the aggressive Scandinavian power in the North. The time was favorable, with disturbed conditions in Sweden, and a youth of eighteen without experience upon the throne. The Tsar, who had recently returned from abroad and had settled matters with his Streltsui in Moscow, saw in this enterprise just the opportunity he desired, and joined the coalition.

At the Battle of Narva (1700) there were two surprises: one when Peter found that he knew almost nothing about the art of warfare, and the other when it was revealed to Charles XII. that he was a military genius and his natural vocation was that of a conqueror. But if Charles was intoxicated by his enormous success, Peter accepted his humiliating defeat almost gratefully as a harsh lesson in military art. The sacrifice of men had been terrible, but the lesson was not lost. The next year there were small Russian victories, and these crept nearer and nearer to the Baltic, until at last the river upon which the great Nevski won his surname was reached—and the Neva was his! Peter lost no time. He personally superintended the building of a fort and then a church which were to be the nucleus of a city; and there may be seen in St. Petersburg to-day the little hut in which lived the Tsar while he was founding the capital which bears his name (1703). No wonder it seemed a wild project to build the capital of an empire, not only on its frontier, but upon low marshy ground subject to the encroachments of the sea from which it had only half emerged; and in a latitude where for two months of the year the twilight and the dawn meet and there is no night, and where for two other months the sun rises after nine in the morning and sets before three. Not only must he build a city, but create the dry land for it to stand upon; and it is said that six hundred acres have been reclaimed from the sea at St. Petersburg since it was founded.

Charles XII. was too much occupied to care for these insignificant events. He sent word that when he had time he would come and burn down Peter's wooden town. He was leading a victorious army toward Poland, he had beheaded the traitorous Patkul, and everything was bowing before him. The great Marlborough was suing for his aid in the coalition against Louis XIV. in the War of the Spanish Succession. Flushed with victory, Charles felt that the fate of Europe was lying in his hands. He had only to decide in which direction to move—whether to help to curb the ambition of the Grand Monarque in the West, or to carry out his first design of crushing the rising power of the Great Autocrat in the East. He preferred the latter. The question then arose whether to enter Russia by the North or by way of Poland, where he was now master. The scale was turned probably by learning that the Cossacks in Little Russia were growing impatient and were ripe for rebellion against the Tsar.

Peter was anxious to prevent the invasion. He had a wholesome admiration for the terrible Swedish army, not much confidence in his own, and his empire was in disorder. He sent word to Charles that he would be satisfied to withdraw from the West if he could have one port on the Baltic. The king's haughty reply was: "Tell your Tsar I will treat with him in Moscow," to which Peter rejoined: "My brother Charles wants to play the part of an Alexander, but he will not find in me a Darius."

It is possible that upon Ivan Mazeppa, who was chief or Hetman of the Cossacks at this time, rests the responsibility of the crushing defeat which terminated the brilliant career of Charles XII. Mazeppa was the Polish gentleman whose punishment at the hands of an infuriated husband has been the subject of poems by Lord Byron and Pushkin, and also of a painting by Horace Vernet. This picturesque traitor, who always rose upon the necks of the people who trusted him, whose friendships he one after another invariably betrayed, reached a final climax of infamy by offering to sacrifice the Tsar, the friend who believed in him so absolutely that he sent into exile or to death anyone who questioned his fidelity. Mazeppa had been with Peter at Azof, and abundant honors were waiting for him; but he was dazzled by the career of the Swedish conqueror, and believed he might rise higher under Charles XII. than under his rough, imperious master at Moscow. So he wrote the King that he might rely upon him to join him with 40,000 Cossacks in Little Russia. He thought it would be an easy matter to turn the irritated Cossacks from the Tsar. They were restive under the severity of the new military régime, and also smarting under a decree forbidding them to receive any more fugitive peasants fleeing from serfdom. But he had miscalculated their lack of fidelity and his own power over them.

It was this fatal promise, which was never to be kept, that probably lured Charles to his ruin. After a long and disastrous campaign he met his final crushing defeat at Poltova in 1709. The King and Mazeppa, companions in flight, together entered the Sultan's dominions as fugitives, and of the army before which a short time ago Europe had trembled—there was left not one battalion.

The Baltic was passing into new hands. "The window" opening upon the West was to become a door, and the key of the door was to be kept upon the side toward Russia! Sweden, which under Gustavus Adolphus, Charles XI., and Charles XII. had played such a glorious part, was never to do it again; and the place she had left vacant was to be filled by a new and greater Power. Russia had dispelled the awakened dream of a great Scandinavian Empire and—so long excluded and humiliated—was going to make a triumphal entry into the family of European nations.

The Tsar, with his innovations and reforms, was vindicated. For breadth of design and statesmanship there was not one sovereign in the coalition who could compare with this man who, Bishop Burnet thought, was better fitted for a mechanic than a Prince—and "incapable of a great enterprise."

Of Charles XII. it has been said that "he was a hero of the Scandinavian Edda set down in the wrong century," and again that he was the last of the Vikings, and of the Varangian Princes. But Mazeppa said of him, when dying in exile: "How could I have been seduced in my old age by a military vagabond!"

Ivan, Peter's infirm brother and associate upon the throne, had died in 1696. Another oppressive tie had also been severed. He had married at seventeen Eudoxia, belonging to a proud conservative Russian family. He had never loved her, and when she scornfully opposed his policy of reform, she became an object of intense aversion. After his triumph at Azof, he sent orders that the Tsaritsa must not be at the palace upon his return, and soon thereafter she was separated from her child Alexis, placed in a monastery, and finally divorced. At the surrender of Marienburg in Livonia (1702) there was among the captives the family of a Lutheran pastor named Glück. Catherine, a young girl of sixteen, a servant in the family, had just married a Swedish soldier, who was killed the following day in battle. We would have to look far for a more romantic story than that of this Protestant waiting-maid. Menschikof, Peter's great general, was attracted by her beauty and took the young girl under his protection. But when the Tsar was also fascinated by her artless simplicity, she was transferred to his more distinguished protection. Little did Catherine think when weeping for her Swedish lover in Pastor Glück's kitchen that she was on her way to the throne of Russia. But such was her destiny. She did not know how to write her name, but she knew something which served her better. She knew how to establish an influence possessed by no one else over the strange husband to whom in 1707 she was secretly married.

CHAPTER XVI.RUSSIA KNOUTED INTO CIVILIZATION—PETER DEAD

While Peter was absorbing more territory on the Baltic, and while he was with frenzied haste building his new city, Charles XII. was still hiding in Poland. The Turks were burning with desire to recapture Azof, and the Khan of Tartary had his own revenges and reprisals at heart urging him on; so, at the instigation of Charles and the Khan, the Sultan declared war against Russia in 1710.

It seemed to the Russian people like a revival of their ancient glories when their Tsar, with a great army, was following in the footsteps of the Grand Princes to free the Slav race from its old infidel enemies. Catherine, from whom Peter would not be separated, was to be his companion in the campaign. But the enterprise, so fascinating in prospect, was attended with unexpected disaster and suffering; and the climax was finally reached when Peter was lying ill in his tent, with an army of only 24,000 men about to face one of over 200,000—Tatars and Turks— commanded by skilled generals, adherents of Charles XII. This was probably the darkest hour in Peter's career. The work of his life was about to be overthrown; it seemed as if a miracle could not save him. Someone suggested that the cupidity of the Grand Vizier, Balthazi, was the vulnerable spot. He loved gold better than glory. Two hundred thousand rubles were quickly collected—Catherine throwing in her jewels as an added lure. The shining gold, with the glittering jewels on top, averted the inevitable fate. Balthazi consented to treat for peace upon condition that Charles XII. be permitted to go back to Sweden unmolested, and that Azof be relinquished (Treaty of Pruth). Peter's heart was sorely wrung by giving up Azof, and his fleet, and his outlet to the Southern seas. The peace was costly, but welcome; and Catherine had earned his everlasting gratitude.

The Tsar now returned to the task of reforming his people. There were to be no more prostrations before him: the petitioner must call himself "subject," not "slave," and must stand upright like a man in his presence, even if he had to use his stick to make him do so! The Asiatic caftan and the flowing robes must go along with the beards; the terem, with its "twenty-seven locks," must be abolished; the wives and daughters dragged from their seclusion must be clothed like Europeans. Marriage must not be compelled, and the betrothed might see each other before the wedding ceremony.

If it is difficult to civilize one willing barbarian, what must it have been to compel millions to put on the garment of respectability which they hated! Never before was there such a complete social reorganization, so entire a change in the daily habits of a whole people; and so violently effected. It required a soul of iron and a hand of steel to do it; and it has been well said that Russia was knouted into civilization. A secret service was instituted to see that the changes were adopted, and the knout and the ax were the accompaniment of every reforming edict. This extraordinary man was by main force dragging a sullen and angry nation into the path of progress, and by artificial means trying to accomplish in a lifetime what had been the growth of centuries in other lands. Then there must be no competing authorities—no suns shining near to the Central Sun. The Patriarchate—which, after Nikon's attempt in the reign of his grandfather, had been shorn of authority—was now abolished, and a Holy Synod of his own appointing took its place. For the Sobor or States-General there was substituted a Senate, also of his own appointing. The Streltsui, or militia, was swept out of existence; the military Cossacks were deprived of their Hetman or leader; and a standing army, raised by recruiting, replaced these organizations. Nobility meant service. Every nobleman while he lived must serve the state, and he held his fief only upon condition of such service; while a nobleman who could not read or write in a foreign tongue forfeited his birthright. This was the way Peter fought idleness and ignorance in his land! New and freer municipal organizations were given to the cities, enlarging the privileges of the citizens; schools and colleges were established; the awful punishment for debtors swept away. He was leveling up as well as leveling down—trying to create a great plateau of modern society, in which he alone towered high, rigid, and inexorable.

If the attempt was impossible and against nature, if Peter violated every law of social development by such a monstrous creation of a modern state, what could have been done better? How long would it have taken Russia to grow into modern civilization? And what would it be now if there had not been just such a strange being—with the nature and heart of a barbarian joined with a brain and an intelligence the peer of any in Europe, capable of seeing that the only hope for Russia was by force to convert it from an Asiatic into a European state?

One act bore with extreme severity upon the free peasantry. They were compelled to enroll themselves with the serfs in their Communes, or to be dealt with as vagrants. Peter has been censured for this and also for not extending his reforming broom to the Communes and overthrowing the whole patriarchal system under which they existed—a system so out of harmony with the modern state he was creating. But it seems to the writer rather that he was guided by a sure instinct when he left untouched the one thing in a Slavonic state, which was really Slavonic. He and the long line of rulers behind him had been ruling by virtue of an authority established by aliens. Russia had from the time of Rurik been governed and formed after foreign models. Peter was at least choosing better models than his predecessors. If it was an apparent mistake to build a modern, centralized state in the eighteenth century upon a social organization belonging to the eleventh century, it may be that in so doing, an inspired despot builded wiser than he knew. May it not be that the final regeneration of that land is to come some day, from the leaven of native instincts in her peasantry, which have never been invaded by foreign influences and which have survived all the vicissitudes of a thousand years in Russia?

The Raskolniks, composed chiefly of free peasants and the smaller merchant class, had fled in large numbers from these blasphemous changes—some among the Cossacks, and many more to the forests, hiding from persecution and from this reign of Satan. The more they studied the Apocalypse the plainer became the signs of the times. Satan was being let loose for a period. They had been looking for the coming of Antichrist and now he had come! The man in whom the spirit of Satan was incarnate was Peter the Great. How else could they explain such impious demeanor in a Tsar of Russia—except that he was of Satanic origin, and was the Devil in disguise? By his newly invented census had he not "numbered the people"—a thing expressly forbidden? And his new "calendar," transferring September to January, was it not clearly a trick of Satan to steal the days of the Lord? And his new title Imperator (Emperor), had it not a diabolic sound? And his order to shave, to disfigure the image of God! How would Christ recognize his own at the Last Day?

Hunted like beasts, these people were living in wild communities, dying often by their own hands rather than yield the point of making the sign of the cross with two fingers instead of three—2700 at one time voluntarily perishing in the flames, in a church where they had taken refuge. Peter put an end to their persecution. They were permitted to practice their ancient rites in the cities and to wear beards without molestation, upon condition of paying a double poll-tax.

The millions of Raskolniks in Russia to-day still consider New Russia a creation of the evil one, and the Tsar as Antichrist. They yield a sullen compliance—pray for the Tsar, then in private throw away the handle of door if a heretic has touched it. It is a conservative Slavonic element which every Tsar since Mikhail Romanoff has had to deal with.

Not one of the reforms was more odious to the people than the removal of the capital from Moscow to St. Petersburg. It violated the most sacred feelings of the nation; and many a soul was secretly looking forward to the time when there would be no Peter, and they would return to the shrine of revered associations. But the new city grew in splendor—a city not of wood, to be the prey of conflagrations like Moscow; but of stone, the first Russia had yet possessed. The great Nevski was already there lying in a cathedral bearing his name, and the Cathedral of Sts. Peter and Paul was ready to entomb the future Tsars. And Peter held his court, a poor imitation of Versailles, and gave great entertainments at which the shy and embarrassed ladies in their new costumes kept apart by themselves, and the attempt to introduce the European dances was a very sorry failure. In 1712 Peter planned a visit to Paris, with two ends in view—a political alliance and a matrimonial one. He ardently desired to arrange for the future marriage of his little daughter Elizabeth with Louis XV., the infant King of France. Neither suit was successful, but it is interesting to learn how different was the impression he produced from the one twelve years before. Saint-Simon writes of him: "His manner was at once the most majestic, the proudest, the most sustained, and at the same time the least embarrassing." That he was still eccentric may be judged from his call upon Mme. de Maintenon. She was ill in bed, and could not receive him; but he was not to be baffled. He drew aside the bed-curtains and stared at her fixedly, while she in speechless indignation glared at him. So, without one word, these two historic persons met—and parted! He probably felt curious to see what sort of a woman had enthralled and controlled the policy of Louis XIV. Peter did not intend to subject his wife to the criticism of the witty Frenchwomen, so prudently left her at home.

Charles XII. died in 1718, and in 1721 there was at last peace with Sweden. But the saddest war of all, and one which was never to cease, was that in Peter's own household. His son Alexis, possibly embittered by his mother's fate, and certainly by her influence, grew up into a sullen, morose, and perverse youth. In vain did his father strive to fit him for his great destiny. By no person in the empire—unless, perhaps, his mother—were Peter's reforms more detested than by the son and heir to whom he expected to intrust them. He was in close communication with his mother Eudoxia, who in her monastery, holding court like a Tsaritsa, was surrounded by intriguing and disaffected nobles—all praying for the death of Peter. Every method for reaching the head or heart of this incorrigible son utterly failed. During Peter's absence abroad in 1717, Alexis disappeared. Tolstoi, the Tsar's emissary, after a long search tracked him to his hiding place and induced him to return. There was a terrible scene with his father, who had discovered that his son was more than perverse, he was a traitor—the center of a conspiracy, and in close relations with his enemies at home and abroad, betraying his interests to Germany and to Sweden.

The plan, instigated by Eudoxia, was that Alexis, immediately upon the death of his father—which God was importuned to hasten—should return to Moscow, restore the picturesque old barbarism, abandon the territory on the Baltic, and the infant navy, and the city of his father's love; in other words, that he should scatter to the winds the prodigious results of his father's reign! It was monstrous—and so was its punishment! Eudoxia was whipped and placed in close confinement, and thirty conspirators, members of her "court," were in various ways butchered. Then Alexis, the confessed traitor, was tried by a tribunal at the head of which was Menschikof—and sentenced to death.

On the morning of the 27th of June, 1718, the Tsar summoned his son to appear before nine of the greatest officers of the state. Concerning what happened, the lips of those nine men were forever sealed. But the day following it was announced that Alexis, the son of the emperor, was dead; and it is believed that he died under the knout.

The question of succession now became a very grave one. Alexis, who had under compulsion married Charlotte of Brunswick, left a son Peter. The only other heirs were the Tsar's two daughters Anna and Elizabeth, the children of Catherine. Shortly after the tragedy of his son's death, Peter caused Catherine to be formally crowned Empress, probably in anticipation of his own death, which occurred in 1725.

CHAPTER XVII.GERMINATING OF SEED—CATHERINE EMPRESS

The chief objection to a wise and beneficent despotism is that its creator is not immortal. The trouble with the Alexanders and the Charlemagnes and the Peters is that the span of human life is too short for their magnificent designs, which fall, while incomplete, into incompetent or vicious hands, and the work is overthrown. Peter's rest in his mausoleum at Sts. Peter and Paul must have been uneasy if he saw the reigns immediately succeeding his own. Not one man capable of a lofty patriotism like his, not one man working with unselfish energy for Russia; but, just as in the olden time, oligarchic factions with leaders striving for that cause which would best protect and elevate themselves. Menschikof, Apraxin, Tolstoi promoting the cause of Catherine that they may not suffer for the death sentence passed upon Alexis; Galitsuin and others seeing their interests in the succession of Peter, son of Alexis and grandson of the Emperor.

Catherine's harmless reign was over in two years (1727) and was followed by another, equally brief and harmless, by the young Peter II. The wily Menschikof succeeded in betrothing his daughter to the young Emperor, but not in retaining his ascendency over the self-willed boy.

We wonder if Peter saw his great minister scheming for wealth and for power, and then his fall, like Wolsey's, from his pinnacle. We wonder if he saw him with his own hands building his hut on the frozen plains of Siberia, clothed, not in rich furs and jewels, but bearded and in long, coarse, gray smock-frock; his daughter, the betrothed of an Emperor, clad, not in ermine, but in sheep-skin. Perhaps the lesson with his master the Carpenter of Saardam served him in building his own shelter in that dread abode. Nor was he alone. He had the best of society, and at every turn of the wheel at St. Petersburg it had aristocratic recruits. The Galitsuins and the Dolgorukis would have joined him soon had they not died in prison, and many others had they not been broken on the wheel or beheaded by Anna, the coarse and vulgar woman who succeeded Peter II., when he suddenly died in 1730.

Anna Ivanovna was the daughter of Peter's brother Ivan V., who was associated with him upon the throne. She had the force to defeat an oligarchic attempt to tie her hands. The plan had originated with the Galitsuins and Dolgorukis, and was really calculated to benefit the state in a period of incompetent or vicious rulers by having the authority of the Crown limited by a council of eight ministers. But it was reactionary. It was introducing a principle which had been condemned, and was a veiled attempt to undo the work of the Ivans and the Romanoffs, and to place the real power as of old in the hands of ruling families. The plan fell, and the leaders fell with it, and a host of their followers. The executioners were busy at St. Petersburg, and the aristocratic colony in Siberia grew larger.

Anna's reign was the period of a preponderating German influence in politics and at court. Germans held high positions; one of them, Gustav Biron, the highest and most influential of all. Anna's infatuation for this man made him the ruling spirit in her reign and the Regent in the next, until he had his turn in disgrace and exile. Added to the dissatisfaction on account of German ascendency was a growing feeling that the succession should come through Peter, instead of through Ivan, his insignificant associate upon the throne. Such was the prevailing sentiment at the time of Anna's death (1740). The Tsaritsa named Ivan, a grand-nephew, the infant son of her niece Anna, her successor under the Regency of Biron, the man who had controlled the policy of the administration during her reign.

This was only a brief and tragic episode. Biron was swiftly swept out of power and into exile, and succeeded in the Regency by Anna, the mother of the infant Emperor; then, following quickly upon that, was a carefully matured conspiracy formed in the interest of Elizabeth Petrovna, the beautiful daughter whose marriage with the young Louis XV. had been an object of the great Peter's hopes.

In this connection it is well to mention that the terminations vich and vna, so constantly met in Russian names, have an important significance—vich meaning son of, and vna daughter of. Elizabeth Petrovna is Elizabeth the daughter of Peter, and Peter Alexievich is Peter the son of Alexis. In like manner Tsarevich and Tsarevna are respectively the son and daughter of the Tsar; Czar, Czarevich, and Czarevna being the modern form, and Czarina instead of Tsaritsa. The historian may for convenience omit the surname thus created, but in Russia it would be a great breach of decorum to do so.

By a sudden coup d'état, Elizabeth Petrovna took her rightful place upon the throne of her father (1741). In the dead of night the unfortunate Anna and her husband were awakened, carried into exile, and their infant son Ivan VI. was immured in a prison, where he was to grow up to manhood,—shattered in mind by his horrible existence of twenty years,—and then to be mercifully put out of the way as a possible menace to the ambitious plans of a woman.

Of the heads that dropped by orders of Elizabeth it is needless to speak; but of one that was spared there is an interesting account. Ostermann, a German, had been vice chancellor to the Empress Anna, and had also brought about the downfall of Biron the Regent. Now his turn had come. He was taken to the place of execution with the rest; his gray head was laid upon the block, his collar unbuttoned and gown drawn back by the executioner—when a reprieve was announced. Her Gracious Majesty was going to permit him to go to Siberia. He arose, bowed, said: "I pray you give me back my wig," calmly put it on the head he had not lost, buttoned his shirt, replaced his gown, and started to join his company of friends—and of enemies—in exile.

Elizabeth was a vain voluptuary. If any glory attaches to her reign it came from the stored energies left by her great father. The marvel is that in this succession of vicious and aimless tyrannies by shameless women and incompetent men, Russia did not fall into anarchy and revolution. But nothing was undone. The dignity of Moscow was preserved by the fact that the coronations must take place there. But there was no longer a reactionary party scheming for a return to the Ancient City. The seed scattered by Peter had everywhere taken hold upon the soil, and now began to burst into flower. A university was founded at Moscow. St. Petersburg was filled with French artists and scholars, and had an Academy of Art and of Science, which the great Voltaire asked permission to join, while conferring with Ivan Shuvalof over the History of

Peter the Great which he was then engaged in writing. There were no more ugly German costumes; French dress, manners and speech were the fashion. Russia was assimilating Europe: it had tried Holland under Peter, then Germany under Empress Anna; but found its true affinity with France under Elizabeth, when to write and speak French like a Parisian became the badge of high station and culture.

So of its own momentum Russia had moved on without one strong competent personality at its head, and had become a tremendous force which must be reckoned with by the nations of Europe. In every great political combination the important question was, on which side she would throw her immense weight; and Elizabeth was courted and flattered to her heart's content by foreign diplomatists and their masters. Frederick the Great had reason to regret that he had been witty at her expense. It was almost his undoing by turning the scale against him at a critical moment. Elizabeth did not forget it and had her revenge when she joined Maria Theresa in the final struggle with Frederick in 1757. And Frederick also remembered it in 1760, when, as he dramatically expressed it, "The Barbarians were in Berlin engaged in digging the grave of humanity."

But all benefit from these enormous successes was abandoned, when the commanding Russian officer Apraxin mysteriously withdrew and returned with his army to Russia. This was undoubtedly part of a deeply laid plot of which Frederick was cognizant, and working in concert with a certain distinguished lady in Elizabeth's own court—a clever puller of wires who was going to fill some important chapters in Russian history!

The Empress had chosen for her successor her nephew Peter, son of her only sister and the Duke of Holstein. The far-seeing Frederick had brought about a marriage between this youth and a German Princess, Sophia of Anhalt-Zerbst. Then the Future Emperor Peter III. and his German bride took up their abode in the palace at St. Petersburg, she having been rechristened Catherine, upon adopting the Greek faith. A mutual dislike deepened into hatred between this brilliant, clever woman and her vulgar and inferior husband; and there is little doubt that the treacherous conduct of the Russian commander was part of a plan to place her infant son Paul upon the throne instead of his father, and make her Regent. Elizabeth's death was apparently at hand and the general mistrust of Peter's fitness for the position opened the way for such a conspiracy— which, however, is not known, but only suspected.

The one merciful edict which adorns this reign is the "abolishing of the death penalty." But as the knout became more than ever active, we are left to infer that by a nice distinction in the Russian mind death under that instrument of torture was not considered "capital punishment."

It is said that when the daughter of the austere Peter died, she left sixteen thousand dresses, thousands of slippers, and two large chests of silk stockings—a wardrobe which would have astonished her mother at the time she was serving the table of the Pastor Glück. Elizabeth expired in 1761, and the throne passed to Peter III., grandson of Peter the Great and Catherine I.

The first act of the new Tsar was a delightful surprise to the nobility. He published a manifesto freeing the nobles from the obligation of service imposed by Peter the Great, saying that this law, which was wise at the time it was enacted, was no longer necessary, now that the nobility was enlightened and devoted to the service of their ruler. The grateful nobles talked of erecting a statue of gold to this benign sovereign, who in like manner abolished the Secret Court of Police and proclaimed pardon to thousands of political fugitives. The Birons were recalled from Siberia, and the old Duke of Kurland and his wife came back like shades from another world, after twenty years of exile.

But this pleasant prelude was very brief. The nobles soon found that their golden idol would have to be made instead of very coarse clay. Nothing could exceed the grossness and the unbalanced folly of Peter's course. He reversed the whole attitude of the state toward Germany. So abject was his devotion to Frederick the Great that he restored to him the Russian conquests, and reached the limit which could be borne when he shouted at one of his orgies: "Let us drink to the health of our King and master Frederick. You may be assured if he should order it, I would make war on hell with all my empire." He was also planning to rid himself of Catherine and to disinherit her child Paul in favor of Ivan VI.; and with this in view that unfortunate youth, who after his twenty years' imprisonment was a mental wreck, was brought to St. Petersburg.

Catherine's plans were carefully laid and then swiftly executed. The Emperor was arrested and his abdication demanded. He submitted as quietly as a child. Catherine writes: "I then sent the deposed Emperor in the care of Alexis Orlof and some gentle and reasonable men to a palace fifteen miles from Peterhof, a secluded spot, but very pleasant."

In four days it was announced that the late Emperor had "suddenly died of a colic to which he was subject." It is known that he was visited by Alexis Orlof and another of Catherine's agents in his "pleasant" retreat, who saw him privately; that a violent struggle was heard in his room; and that he was found lying dead with the black and blue mark of a colossal hand on his throat. That the hand was Orlof's is not doubted; but whether acting under orders from Catherine or not will never be known.

This is what is known as the "Revolution of 1762," which placed Catherine II. upon the throne of Russia. Her son Paul was only six years old; and in less than two years Ivan VI., the only claimant to the throne who could become the center of a conspiracy against her authority, was most opportunely removed. It was said that his guards killed him to prevent an attempted rescue. No one knows or ever will know whether or not Catherine was implicated in his "taking off." But certainly nothing at the time could have pleased her better.

CHAPTER XVIII.PARTITION OF POLAND—DEATH OF CATHERINE

European diplomacy at this period was centered about the perishing state of Poland. That kingdom, once so powerful, was becoming every year more enfeebled.

It was a defective social organization and an arrogant nobility that ruined Poland. There existed only two classes—nobles and serfs. The business and trade of the state were in the hands of Germans and Jews, and there existed no national or middle class in which must reside the life of a modern state. In other words, Poland was patriarchal and mediaeval. She had become unsuited to her environment. Surrounded by powerful absolutisms which had grown out of the ruins of mediaeval forces, she in the eighteenth century was clinging to the traditions of feudalism as if it were still the twelfth century. It was in vain that her sons were patriotic, in vain that they struggled for reforms, in vain that they lay down and died upon battlefields. She alone in Europe had not been borne along on that great wave of centralization long ago, and she had missed an essential experience. She was out of step with the march of civilization, and the advancing forces were going to run over her.

The more enlightened Poles began too late to strive for a firm hereditary monarchy, and to try to curb the power of selfish nobles. Not only was their state falling to pieces within, but it was being crushed from without. Protestant Prussia in the West, Greek Russia in the East, and Catholic Austria on the South, each preparing to absorb all it could get away—not from Poland, but from each other. It was obvious that it was only a question of time when the feeble kingdom wedged in between these powerful and hungry states must succumb; and for Russia, Austria, and Prussia it was simply a question as to the share which should fall to each.

Such was the absorbing problem which employed Catherine's powers from the early years of her reign almost to its close. Europe soon saw that it was a woman of no ordinary ability who was sitting on the throne of Russia. In her foreign policy, and in the vigor infused into the internal administration of her empire, the master-hand became apparent.

As a counter-move to her designs upon Poland, the Turks were induced to harass her by declaring war upon Russia. There was a great surprise in store for Europe as well as for the Ottoman Empire. This dauntless woman was unprepared for such an emergency; but she wrote to one of her generals: "The Romans did not concern themselves with the number of their enemies; they only asked, 'Where are they?'" Her armies swept the Peninsula clear of Tatars and of Turks, and in 1771 a Russian fleet was on the Black Sea, and the terror of Constantinople knew no bounds. If affairs in Europe and disorders in her own empire had not been so pressing, the long-cherished dream of the Grand Princes might have been realized.

A plague in Moscow broke out in 1771 which so excited the superstitions of the people, that it led to an insurrection; immediately following this, a terrible demoralization was created in the South by an illiterate Cossack named Pugatchek, who announced that he was Peter the Third. He claimed that instead of dying as was supposed, he had escaped to the Ukraine, and was now going to St. Petersburg with an army to punish his wife Catherine and to place his son Paul upon the throne. As a pretender he was not dangerous, but as a rallying point for unhappy serfs and for an exasperated and suffering people looking for a leader, he did become a very formidable menace, which finally developed into a Peasants' War. The insurrection was at last quelled, and ended with the execution of the false Peter at Moscow.

In the midst of these distractions at home, while fighting the Ottoman Empire for the shores of the Black Sea, and all Europe over a partition of Poland, the Empress was at the same time introducing reforms in every department of her incoherent and disordered empire. Peter the Great had abolished the Patriarchate. She did more. The monasteries and the ecclesiastical estates, which were exempt from taxes during all the period of Mongol dominion, had never paid tribute to Khans, had in consequence grown to be enormously wealthy. It is said the clergy owned a million serfs. Catherine placed the property of the Church under the administration of a secular commission, and the heads of the monasteries and the clergy were converted from independent sovereigns into mere pensioners of the Crown. Then she assailed the receiving of bribes, and other corrupt practices in the administration of justice. She struggled hard to let in the light of better instruction upon the upper and middle classes. If she could, she would have abolished ignorance and cruelty in the land, not because she was a philanthropist, but because she loved civilization. It was her intellect, not her heart, that made Catherine a reformer. When she severely punished and forever disgraced a lady of high rank for cruelty to her serfs,—forty of whom had been tortured to death,—it was because she had the educated instincts of a European, not an Asiatic, and she had also the intelligence to realize that no state could be made sound which rested upon a foundation of human misery. She established a Russian Academy modeled after the French, its object being to fix the rules for writing and speaking the Russian language and to promote the study of Russian history. In other words, Catherine was a reformer fully in sympathy with the best methods prevailing in Western Europe. She was profoundly interested in the New Philosophy and the intellectual movement in France, was in correspondence with Voltaire and the Encyclopedists, and a student of the theories of Rousseau.

Of course the influence exerted by French genius over Russian civilization at this time did not penetrate far below the upper and highly educated class; but there is no doubt it left a deep impress upon the literature and art of the nation, and also modified Russian characteristics by introducing religious tolerance and habits of courtesy, besides making aspirations after social justice and political liberty entirely respectable. Catherine's "Book of Instructions" to the commission which was created by her to assist in making a new code of laws contained political maxims which would satisfy advanced reformers to-day; although when she saw later that the French Revolution was their logical conclusion, she repudiated them, took Voltaire's bust down from its pedestal, and had it thrown into a rubbish heap. The work she was accomplishing for Russia was second only to that of Peter the Great; and when she is reproached for not having done more and for not having broken the chains forged by Boris upon twenty million people, let it be remembered that she lived in the eighteenth, and not the nineteenth, century; and that at that very time Franklin and Jefferson were framing a constitution which sanctioned the existence of negro slavery in an ideal republic!

A new generation had grown up in Poland, men not nobles nor serfs, but a race of patriots familiar with the stirring literature of their century. They had seen their land broken into fragments and then ground fine by a proud and infatuated nobility. They had seen their pusillanimous kings one after another yielding to the insolent demands for their territory. Polish territory extended eastward into the Ukraine; now that must be cut off and dropped into the lap of Russia. Another arm extended north, separating Eastern Prussia from Western. That too must be cut off and fall to Prussia. Then after shearing these extremities, the Poland which was left must not only accept the spoliation, but co-operate with her despoilers in adopting under their direction a constitution suited to its new humiliation. Her King was making her the laughing-stock of Europe—but before long the name Poland was to become another name for tragedy. Kosciusko had fought in the War of the American Revolution. When he returned, with the badge of the Order of the Cincinnati upon his breast and filled with dreams of the regeneration of his own land by the magic of this new political freedom, he was the chosen leader of the patriots.

The partition of Poland was not all accomplished at one time. It took three repasts to finish the banquet (the partitions of 1792-1793-1794), and then some time more was required to sweep up the fragments and to efface its name from the map of Europe. Kosciusko and his followers made their last vain and desperate stand in 1794, and when he fell covered with wounds at the battle of Kaminski, Poland fell with him. The Poles were to survive only as a more or less unhappy element among nations where they were aliens. Their race affinities were with Russia, for they were a Slavonic people; their religious affinities were with Catholic Austria; but with Protestant Prussia there was not one thing in common, and that was the bitterest servitude of all. The Poles in Russia were to some extent autonomous. They were permitted to continue their local governments under a viceroy appointed by the Tsar; their Slavonic system of communes was not disturbed, nor their language nor customs. Still it was only a privileged servitude after all, and the time was coming when it was to become an unmitigated one. But effaced as a political sovereignty, Poland was to survive as a nationality of genius. Her sons were going to sing their songs in other lands, but Mickiewiz and Sienkiewicz and Chopin are Polish, not Russian.

The alliance of the three sovereigns engaged in this dismemberment was about as friendly as is that of three dogs who have run down a hare and are engaged in picking nice morsels from its bones. If Russia was getting more than her share, the Turks would be incited by Austria or Prussia to attack her in the South; and many times did Catherine's armies desert Poland to march down and defend the Crimea, and her new fort at Sebastopol, and her fleet on the Black Sea. In 1787, accompanied by her grandsons, the Grand Dukes Alexander and Constantine, she made that famous journey down the Dnieper; visited the ancient shrines about Kief; stood in the picturesque old capital of Saraï, on the spot where Russian Grand Princes had groveled at the feet of the Khans; and then, looked upon Sebastopol, which marked the limit of the new frontier which she had created.

The French Revolution caused a revulsion in her political theories. She indulged in no more abstractions about human rights, and had an antipathy for the new principles which had led to the execution of the King and Queen and to such revolting horrors. She made a holocaust of the literature she had once thought entertaining. Russians suspected of liberal tendencies were watched, and upon the slightest pretext sent to Siberia, and she urged the King of Sweden to head a crusade against this pestilential democracy, which she would help him to sweep out of Europe. It was Catherine, in consultation with the Emperor of Austria, who first talked of dismembering Turkey and creating out of its own territory a group of neutral states lying between Europe and the Ottoman Empire. And Voltaire's dream of a union of the Greek peoples into an Hellenic kingdom she improved upon by a larger plan of her own, by which she was to be the conqueror of the Ottoman Empire, while her grandson Constantine, sitting on a throne at Constantinople, should rule Greeks and Turks alike under a Russian protectorate.

Upon the private life of Catherine there is no need to dwell. This is not the biography of a woman, but the history of the empire she magnificently ruled for thirty-four years. It is enough to say she was not better than her predecessors, the Tsaritsas Elizabeth and Anna. The influence exerted by Menschikof in the reign of Catherine I., and Biron in that of Anna, was to be exerted by Alexis Orlof, Potemkin, and other favorites in this. Her son Paul, who was apparently an object of dislike, was kept in humiliating subordination to the Orlofs and her other princely favorites, to whose councils he was never invited. Righteousness and moral elevation did not exist in her character nor in her reign; but for political insight, breadth of statesmanship, and a powerful grasp upon the enormous problems in her heterogeneous empire, she is entitled to rank with the few sovereigns who are called "Great." A German by birth, a French-woman by intellectual tastes and tendencies—she was above all else a Russian, and bent all the resources of her powerful personality to the enlightenment and advancement of the land of her adoption. Her people were not "knouted into civilization," but invited and drawn into it. Her touch was terribly firm—but elastic. She was arbitrary, but tolerant; and if her reign was a despotism, it was a despotism of that broad type which deals with the sources of things, and does not bear heavily upon individuals. The Empress Catherine died suddenly in 1796, and Paul I. was crowned Emperor of Russia.

CHAPTER XIX.NAPOLEON IN EUROPE—ATTITUDE OF RUSSIA

Paul was forty-one years old when he ascended the throne he had for twenty years believed was rightfully his. The mystery surrounding the death of his father Peter III., the humiliations he had suffered at his mother's court, and what he considered her usurpation of his rights—all these had been for years fermenting in his narrow brain.

His first act gave vent to his long-smothered indignation and his suspicions regarding his father's death. Peter's remains were exhumed—placed beside those of Catherine lying in state, to share all the honors of her obsequies and to be entombed with her; while Alexis Orlof, his supposed murderer, was compelled to march beside the coffin, bearing his crown.

Then when Paul had abolished from the official language the words "society" and "citizen," which his mother had delighted to honor—when he had forbidden the wearing of frock-coats, high collars, and neckties, and refused to allow Frenchmen to enter his territory—and when he had compelled his people to get out of their carriages and kneel in the mud as he passed—he supposed he was strengthening the foundations of authority which Catherine II. had loosened.

To him is attributed the famous saying, "Know that the only person of consideration in Russia is the person whom I address, and he only during the time I am addressing him." He was a born despot, and his reforms consisted in a return to Prussian methods and to an Oriental servility. The policy he announced was one of peace with Europe—a cessation of those wars by which his mother had for thirty-four years been draining the treasury. He was going to turn his conquests toward the East; and vast plans, with vague and indefinite outlines, were forming in the narrow confines of his restless brain. But these were interrupted by unexpected conditions.

In 1796 the military genius of a young man twenty-seven years old electrified Europe. Napoleon Bonaparte, at the head of a ragged, unpaid French army, overthrew Northern Italy, and out of the fragments created a Cisalpine Republic. The possession of the Ionian Isles, quickly followed by the occupation of Egypt, threatened the East. So Turkey and Russia, contrary to all old traditions, formed a defensive alliance, which was quickly followed by an offensive one between Russia and Austria. But the tactics so successful against Poles and Turks were unavailing against those employed by the new Conqueror. The Russian commander Suvorov was defeated and returned in disgrace to his enraged master at St. Petersburg, who refused to receive him. In 1798 Bonaparte had secured Belgium, had compelled Austria to cede to him Lombardy, also to promise him help in getting the left bank of the Rhine from the Germanic body, and to acknowledge his Cisalpine Republic.

The Emperor Paul's feelings underwent a swift change. He was blinded by the glory of Napoleon's conquests and pleased with his despotic methods. He conceived not only a friendship but a passion for the man who could accomplish such things. Austria and England had both offended him, so he readily fell into a plan for a Franco-Russian understanding for mutual benefit, from which there developed a larger plan.

The object of this was the overthrow of British dominion in India. Paul was to move with a large army into Hindostan, there to be joined by a French army from Egypt; then they would together sweep through the country of the Great Mogul, gathering up the English settlements by the way and so placating the native population and Princes that they would join them in the liberation of their country from English tyranny and usurpation. Paul said in his manifesto to the army that the Great Mogul and the Sovereign Princes were to be undisturbed; nothing was to be attacked but the commercial establishments acquired by money and used to oppress and to enslave India. At the same time he said to his army, "The treasures of the Indies shall be your recompense," failing to state how these treasures were to be obtained without disturbing the Sovereign Princes.

It is known that Napoleon had plans of an empire in the East, and it is also known that some compact of this kind did exist between him and the Emperor Paul. In 1801 eleven regiments of Cossacks, the vanguard of the army which was to follow, had started upon the great undertaking, when news was received that the Emperor Paul I. was dead.

The unbalanced course pursued by the Tsar, his unwise reforms, and his capricious policy had not only alienated everyone, but caused serious apprehensions for the safety of the empire. He had arrayed himself against his wife and his children; had threatened to disinherit Alexander, his oldest son and heir, whom he especially hated. A plot was formed to compel his abdication. To that extent his sons Alexander and Constantine were aware of and party to it.

On the night of the 23d of March, 1801, the conspirators entered Paul's sleeping apartment after he had retired, and, sword in hand, presented the abdication for him to sign. There was a struggle in which the lamp was overturned, and in the darkness the Tsar, who had fallen upon the floor, was strangled with an officer's scarf.

On the 24th of March, 1801, Alexander, who was entirely innocent of complicity in this crime, was proclaimed Emperor of Russia.

It is said that when Bonaparte saw the downfall of his vast design, he could not contain his rage; and pointing to England as the instigator of the deed, he said in the Moniteur: "It is for history to clear up the secret of this tragedy, and to say what national policy was interested in such a catastrophe!"

The Emperor Paul had an acute, although narrow, intelligence, and was not without generous impulses. But although he sometimes made impetuous reparation for injury, although he recalled exiles from Siberia and gave to Kosciusko and other patriots their freedom, unless his kindness was properly met the reaction toward severity was excessive. A little leaven of good with much that is evil sometimes creates a very explosive mixture, and converts what would be a mild, even tyranny into a vindictive and revengeful one. When we behold the traits exhibited during this brief reign of five years, we are not surprised at Catherine's unwillingness to resign to her son the empire for which she had done so much; and we are inclined to believe it is true that there was, as has been rumored, a will left by the Empress naming as her heir the grandson whom she had carefully prepared to be her successor, and that this paper was destroyed by the conspirators.

There is one wise act to record in the reign of Paul—although it was probably prompted not by a desire to benefit the future so much as to reverse the past. Peter the Great, probably on account of his perverse son Alexis, had set aside the principle of primogeniture; a principle not Slavonic, but established by the Muscovite Princes. Peter, the ruthless reformer, placed in the hands of the sovereign the power to choose his own successor. Paul reestablished this principle, and thereby bestowed a great benefit upon Russia.

CHAPTER XX.NAPOLEON IN RUSSIA— HOLY ALLIANCE

A youth of twenty-five years was Tsar and Autocrat of All the Russias. Alexander had from his birth been withdrawn entirely from his father's influence. The tutor chosen by his grandmother was Laharpe, a Swiss Republican, and the principles of political freedom were at the foundation of his training. It was of course during the period of her own liberal tendencies that Alexander was imbued with the advanced theories which had captured intellectual Europe in the days before the French Revolution. The new Emperor declared in a manifesto that his reign should be inspired by the aims and principles of Catherine II. He then quickly freed himself from the conspirators who had murdered his father, and drew about him a group of young men like himself, utterly inexperienced, but enthusiastic dreamers of a reign of goodwill which should regenerate Russia. With the utmost confidence, reforms of the most radical nature were proposed and discussed. There was to be a gradual emancipation of the serfs, and misery of all sorts to be lifted from the land by a new and benign system of government which should be representative and constitutional. Many changes were at once instituted. The old system of "colleges," or departments, established by Peter the Great was removed and a group of ministers after the European custom constituted the Tsar's official household, or what would once have been called his Drujina. In the very first year of this reign there began an accession of territory in Asia, which gravitated as if by natural law toward the huge mass. The picturesque old kingdom of Georgia, lying south of the Caucasus between the Black and Caspian seas, was the home of that fair and gifted race which, fallen from its high estate, had become the victim of the Turks, and, with its congener Circassia, had long provided the harems of the Ottoman Empire with beautiful slaves. The Georgians had often appealed to the Tsars for protection, and in 1810 the treaty was signed which incorporated the suffering kingdom with Russia.

A portion of the state passed to Russia in 1801, at the commencement of Alexander's reign; but the formal surrender of the whole by treaty was not until 1810.

So day by day, while the young Emperor and his friends were living in their pleasant Utopia, Russia, with all its incoherent elements, with its vast energies, its vast riches, and its vast miseries, was expanding and assuming a more dominating position in Europe. What would be done at St. Petersburg, was the question of supreme importance; and Alexander was being importuned to join the coalition against the common enemy Bonaparte.

The night before the 2d of October, 1805, the Russian Emperor and his young officers, as confident of victory as they were of their ability to reconstruct Russia, were impatiently waiting for the morrow, and the conflict at Austerlitz. With a ridiculous assurance the young Alexander sent by the young Prince Dolgoruki a note addressed—not to the Emperor—but to the "Head of the French Nation," stating his demands for the abandonment of Italy and immediate peace! Before sundown the next day the "Battle of the Three Emperors" had been fought; the Russian army was scattered after frightful loss, and Alexander, attended by an orderly and two Cossacks, was galloping away as fast as his horse could carry him. Then Napoleon was in Vienna—Francis II. at his bidding took off his imperial crown—the "Confederation of the Rhine" was formed out of Germanic States; and then the terrible and invincible man turned toward Prussia, defeated a Russian army which came to its rescue, and in 1806 was in Berlin—master and arbiter of Europe!

Alexander, the romantic champion of right and justice, the dreamer of ideal dreams, had been carried by the whirlpool of events into currents too strong for him. He stood alone on the continent of Europe face to face with the man who was subjugating it. His army was broken in pieces, and perhaps an invasion of his own empire was at hand. Should he make terms with this man whose career had so revolted him?—or should he defy him and accept the risk of an invasion, which, by offering freedom to the serfs and independence to the Poles, might give the invader the immediate support of millions of his own subjects? Then added to the conflict with his old self, there was the irresistible magic of Napoleon's personal influence. A two-hours' interview on the raft at Tilsit—June 25, 1807—changed the whole direction of Alexander's policy, and made him an ally of the despot he had detested, whom he now joined in determining the fate of Europe. Together they decided who should occupy thrones and who should not; to whom there should be recompense, and who should be despoiled; and the Emperor of Russia consented to join the Emperor of the French in a war upon the commercial prosperity of England—his old friend and ally—by means of a continental blockade.

Times were changed. It was not so long ago—just one hundred years—since Peter the Great had opened one small window for the light from civilized Europe to glimmer through; and now the Tsar of that same Russia, in a two-hours' interview on a raft, was deciding what should be the fate of Europe!

The Emperor's young companions, with small experience and lofty aims, were keenly disappointed in him. This alliance was in contravention of all their ideals. He began to grow distrustful and cold toward them, leaning entirely upon Speranski, his prime minister, who was French in his sympathies and a profound admirer of Napoleon. Alexander, no less zealous for reforms than before, hurt at the defection of his friends and trying to justify himself to himself, said "Does not this man represent the new forces in conflict with the old?" But he was not at ease. He and his minister worked laboriously; a systematic plan of reform was prepared. Speranski considered the Code Napoleon the model of all progressive legislation. Its adoption was desired, but it was suited only to a homogeneous people; it was a modern garment and not to be worn by a nation in which feudalism lingered, in which there was not a perfect equality before the law; hence the emancipation of the serfs must be the corner-stone of the new structure. The difficulties grew larger as they were approached. He had disappointed the friends of his youth, had displeased his nobility, and a general feeling of irritation prevailed upon finding themselves involved by the Franco-Russian alliance in wars with England, Austria, and Sweden, and the prosperity of the empire seriously impaired by the continental blockade. But when Bonaparte began to show scant courtesy to his Russian ally, and to act as if he were his master, then

Alexander's disenchantment was complete. He freed himself from the unnatural alliance, and faced the inevitable consequences.

Napoleon, also glad to be freed from a sentimental friendship not at all to his taste, prepared to carry out his long-contemplated design. In July of 1812, by way of Poland, he entered Russia with an army of over 678,000 souls. It was a human avalanche collected mainly from the people he had conquered, with which he intended to overwhelm the Russian Empire. It was of little consequence that thirty or forty thousand fell as this or that town was captured by the way. He had expected victory to be costly, and on he pressed with diminished numbers toward Moscow, armies retreating and villages burning before him. If St. Petersburg was the brain of Russia, Moscow—Moscow the Holy—was its heart! What should they do? Should they lure the French army on to its destruction and then burn and retreat? or should they there take their stand and sacrifice the last army of Russia to save Moscow? With tears streaming down their cheeks they yielded to the words of Kutuzof, who said: "When it becomes a matter of the salvation of Russia, Moscow is only a city like any other. Let us retreat." The archives and treasures of the churches and palaces were carried to Valdimir, such as could of the people following them, and the city was left to its fate.

On September the 14th, 1812, the French troops defiled through the streets of Moscow singing the Marseillaise, and Napoleon established himself in the ancient palace of the Ivans within the walls of the Kremlin. The torches had been distributed, and were in the hands of the Muscovites. The stores of brandy, and boats loaded with alcohol, were simultaneously ignited, and a fierce conflagration like a sea of flame raged below the Kremlin. Napoleon, compelled to force his way through these volcanic fires himself, narrowly escaped.

For five days they continued, devouring supplies and everything upon which the army had depended for shelter and subsistence. For thirty-five days more they waited among the blackened ruins. All was over with the French conquest. The troops were eating their horses, and thousands were already perishing with hunger. Then the elements began to fight for Russia—the snow-flakes came, then the bitter polar winds, cutting like a razor; and a winding sheet of snow enveloped the land. On the 13th of October, after lighting a mine under the Kremlin, with sullen rage the French troops marched out of Moscow. The Great Tower of Ivan erected by Boris was cracked and some portions of palaces and gateways destroyed by this vicious and useless act of revenge.

Then, instead of marching upon St. Petersburg as he had expected, Napoleon escaped alone to the frontier, leaving his perishing wreck of an army to get back as it could. The peasantry, the mushiks, whom the Russians had feared to trust—infuriated by the destruction of their homes, committed awful atrocities upon the starving, freezing soldiers, who, maddened by cold and hunger and by the singing in their ears of the rarefied air, many of them leaped into the bivouac fires. It was a colossal tragedy. Of the 678,000 soldiers only 80,000 ever returned.

The extinction of the grand army of invasion was complete. But in the following year, with another great army, the indomitable Napoleon was conducting a campaign in Germany which ended with the final defeat at Leipzig—then the march upon Paris—and in March, 1814,

Alexander at the head of the Allies was in the French capital, dictating the terms of surrender. This young man had played the most brilliant part in the great drama of Liberation. He was hailed as a Deliverer, and exerted a more powerful influence than any of the other sovereigns, in the long period required for rearranging Europe after the passing of Napoleon—the disturber of the peace of the world.

In 1809 Sweden had surrendered to Russia Finland, which had belonged to that country for six centuries. The kindly-intentioned Alexander conceded to the Finns many privileges similar to those enjoyed by Poland, which until recent years have not been seriously interfered with. He guaranteed to them a Diet, a separate army, and the continuance of their own language and customs. A ukase just issued by the present emperor seriously invades these privileges, and a forcible Russification of Finland threatens to bring a wave of Finnish emigration to America (1899).

When the Emperor Alexander returned after the Treaty of Paris he was thirty-four years old. Many of the illusions of his youth had faded. His marriage with Elizabeth of Baden was unhappy. His plans for reform had not been understood by the people whom they were intended to benefit. He had yielded finally to the demands of his angry nobility, had dismissed his liberal adviser Speranski and substituted Araktcheef, an intolerant, reactionary leader. He grew morose, gloomy, and suspicious, and a reign of extreme severity under Araktcheef commenced. In 1819 he consented to join in a league with Austria and Prussia for the purpose of suppressing the very tendencies he himself had once promoted. The League was called the "Holy Alliance," and its object was to reinstate the principle of the divine right of Kings and to destroy democratic tendencies in the germ. Araktcheef's severities, directed against the lower classes and the peasantry, produced more serious disorders than had yet developed. There were popular uprisings, and in 1823 at Kief there was held secretly a convention at which the people were told that "the obstacle to their liberties was the Romanoff dynasty. They must shrink from nothing—not from the murder of the Emperor, nor the extermination of the Imperial family." The peasants were promised freedom if they would join in the plot, and a definite time was proposed for the assassination of Alexander when he should inspect the troops in the Ukraine in 1824.

When the Tsar heard of this conspiracy in the South he exclaimed: "Ah, the monsters! And I planned for nothing but their happiness!" He brooded over his lost illusions and his father's assassination. His health became seriously disordered, and he was advised to go to the South for change of climate. At Taganrog, on the 1st of December, 1825, he suddenly expired. Almost his last words were: "They may say of me what they will, but I have lived and shall die republican." A statement difficult to accept, regarding a man who helped to create the "Holy Alliance."

CHAPTER XXI.RUSSIA ORIENTALIZED—EASTERN QUESTION

As Alexander left no sons, by the law of primogeniture his brother Constantine, the next oldest in the family of Paul I., should have been his successor. But Constantine had already privately renounced the throne in favor of his brother Nicholas. The actual reason for this renunciation was the Grand Duke's deep attachment to a Polish lady for whom he was willing even to relinquish a crown. The letter announcing his intention contained these words: "Being conscious that I have neither genius, talents, nor energy necessary for my elevation, I beg your Imperial Majesty to transfer this right to my brother Nicholas, the next in succession." The document accepting the renunciation and acknowledging Nicholas as his successor was safely deposited by Alexander, its existence remaining a profound secret even to Nicholas himself.

At the time of the Emperor's death Constantine, who was Viceroy of Poland, was residing at Cracow. Nicholas, unaware of the circumstances, immediately took the oath of allegiance to his brother and also administered it to the troops at St. Petersburg. It required some time for Constantine's letter to arrive, stating his immovable determination to abide by the decision which would be found in his letter to the late Emperor. There followed a contest of generosity— Nicholas urging and protesting, and his brother refusing the elevation. Three weeks passed— weeks of disastrous uncertainty—with no acknowledged head to the Empire.

Such an opportunity was not to be neglected by the revolutionists in the South nor their co-workers in the North. Pestel, the leader, had long been organizing his recruits, and St. Petersburg and Moscow were the centers of secret political societies. The time for action had unexpectedly come. There must be a swift overturning: the entire imperial family must be destroyed, and the Senate and Holy Synod must be compelled to adopt the Constitution which had been prepared.

The hour appointed for the beginning of this direful programme was the day when the senators and the troops should assemble to take the oath of allegiance to Nicholas. The soldiers, who knew nothing of the plot, were incited to refuse to take the oath on the ground that Constantine's resignation was false, and that he was a prisoner and in chains. Constantine was their friend and going to increase their pay. One Moscow regiment openly shouted: "Long life to Constantine!" and when a few conspirators cried "Long live the Constitution!" the soldiers asked if that was Constantine's wife. So the ostensible cause of the revolt, which soon became general, was a fidelity to their rightful Emperor, who was being illegally deposed. Under this mask worked Pestel and his co-conspirators, composed in large measure of men of high intelligence and standing, including even government officials and members of the aristocracy.

A few days were sufficient to overcome this abortive attempt at revolution in Russia. Pestel, when he heard his death sentence, said, "My greatest error is that I tried to gather the harvest before sowing the seed"; and Ruileef, "I knew this enterprise would be my destruction—but could no longer endure the sight of my country's anguish under despotism." When we think of the magnitude of the offense, the monstrous crime which was contemplated; and when we remember that Nicholas was by nature the very incarnation of unrestrained authority, the punishment seems comparatively light. There was no vindictiveness, no wholesale slaughter. Five leaders were deliberately and ignominiously hanged, and hundreds of their misguided followers and sympathizers went into perpetual exile in Siberia—there to expiate the folly of supposing that a handful of inexperienced enthusiasts and doctrinaires could in their studies create new and ideal conditions, and build up with one hand while they were recklessly destroying with the other. Their aims were the abolition of serfdom, the destruction of all existing institutions, and a perfect equality under a constitutional government. They were definite and sweeping—and so were the means for accomplishing them. Their benign government was going to rest upon crime and violence. We should call these men Nihilists now. There were among them writers and thinkers, noble souls which, under the stress of oppression and sympathy, had gone astray. They had failed, but they had proved that there were men in Russia capable of dying for an ideal. When the cause had its martyrs it had become sacred—and though it might sleep, it would not die.

The man sitting upon the throne of Russia now was not torn by conflicts between his ideals and inexorable circumstance. His natural instincts and the conditions of his empire both pointed to the same simple course—an unmitigated autocracy—an absolute rule supported by military power. Instead of opening wider the doors leading into Europe, he intended to close them, and if necessary even to lock them. Instead of encouraging his people to be more European, he was going to be the champion of a new Pan-Slavism and to strive to intensify the Russian national traits. The time had come for this great empire to turn its face away from the West and toward the East, where its true interests were. Such a plan may not have been formulated by Nicholas, but such were the policies instinctively pursued from the beginning of his reign to its close.

Such an attitude naturally brought him at once into conflict with Turkey, with which country he was almost immediately at war. Of course no one suspected him of sentimental sympathy when he espoused the cause of Greece in the picturesque struggle with the Turks which brought Western Europe at last to her rescue. It was only a part of a much larger plan, and when Nicholas had proclaimed himself the Protector of the Orthodox Christians in the East, he had placed himself in a relation to the Eastern Question which could be held by no other sovereign in Europe; for persecuted Christians in the East were not Catholic but Orthodox; and was not he the head of the Orthodox Church? It was to secure this first move in the game of diplomacy that Russia joined England and France, and placed the struggling little state of Greece upon its feet in 1832.

But the conditions in Western Europe were unfavorable to the tranquil pursuit of autocratic ends. Charles X. had presumed too far upon the patient submission of the French people. In 1830 Paris was in a state of insurrection; Charles, the last of the Bourbons, had abdicated; and Louis Philippe, under a new liberal Constitution approved by the people, was King of the French. The indignation of Nicholas at this overturning was still greater when the epidemic of revolt spread to Belgium and to Italy, and then leaped, as such epidemics will, across the intervening space to

Russian Poland. The surface calm in that unhappy state ruled by the Grand Duke Constantine swiftly vanished and revealed an entire people waiting for the day when, at any cost, they might make one more stand for freedom. The plan was a desperate one. It was to assassinate Constantine, who had relinquished a throne rather than leave them; to induce Lithuania, their old ally, to join them; and to create an independent Polish state which would bar the Russians from entering Europe.

In 1831 the brief struggle was ended, and Europe had received the historic announcement, "Order reigns at Warsaw." Not only Warsaw, but Poland, was at the feet of the Emperor. Confiscations, imprisonments, and banishments to Siberia were the least terrible of the punishments. Every germ of a Polish nationality was destroyed—the army and the Diet effaced, Russian systems of taxes, justice, and coinage, and the metric system of weights and measures used in Russia were introduced,—the Julian Calendar superseded the one adopted all over the world—the University of Warsaw was carried to Moscow, and the Polish language was prohibited to be taught in the schools. Indemnity and pardon were offered to those who abjured the Roman Catholic faith, and many were received into the bosom of the National Orthodox Church; those refusing this offer of clemency being subjected to great cruelties. Poland was no more. Polish exiles were scattered all over Europe. In France, Hungary, Italy, wherever there were lovers of freedom, there were thousands of these emigrants without a country, living illustrations of what an unrestrained despotism might do, and everywhere intensifying the desires of patriots to achieve political freedom in their own lands.

Nicholas, as the chief representative of conservatism in Europe, looked upon France with especial aversion. Paris was the center of these pernicious movements which periodically shook Europe to its foundations. It had overthrown his ally Charles X., and had been the direct cause of the insurrection in Poland which had cost him thousands of rubles and lives; and now nowhere else was such sympathetic welcome given to the Polish refugees, thousands of whom were in the French army. His relations with Louis Philippe became strained, and he was looking about for an opportunity to manifest his ill will. In the meantime he addressed himself to what he considered the reforms in his own empire. He was going to establish a sort of political quarantine to keep out European influences. It was forbidden to send young men to Western universities—the term of absence in foreign countries was limited to five years for nobles, three for Russian subjects. The Russian language, literature, and history were to be given prominence over all studies in the schools. German free-thought was especially disliked by him. His instincts were not mistaken, for what the Encyclopedists had been to the Revolution of 1789, the new school of thought in Germany would be to that of 1848. So from his point of view he was wise in excluding philosophy from the universities and permitting it to be taught only by ecclesiastics.

The Khedive of Egypt, who ruled under a Turkish protectorate, in 1832 was at war with his master the Sultan. It suited the Emperor of Russia at this time to do the Sultan a kindness, so he joined him in bringing the Khedive to terms, and as his reward received a secret promise from the Porte to close the Dardanelles in case of war against Russia—to permit no foreign warships to pass through upon any pretext. There was indignation in Europe when this was known, and out of the whole imbroglio there came just what Nicholas and his minister Nesselrode had intended—a joint protection of Turkey by the Great Powers, from which France was excluded on account of her avowed sympathy for the Khedive in the recent troubles.

The great game of diplomacy had begun. Nicholas, for the sake of humiliating France, had allied himself with England, his natural enemy, and had assumed the part of Protector of an Ottoman integrity which he more than anyone else had tried to destroy! There were to be many strange roles played in this Eastern drama—many surprises for Christendom; and for Nicholas the surprise of a crushing defeat a few years later to which France contributed, possibly in retaliation for this humiliation.

The Ottoman Empire had reached its zenith in 1550 under Suleyman the Magnificent, when, with its eastern frontier in the heart of Asia, its European frontier touching Russia and Austria, it held in its grasp Egypt, the northern coast of Africa, and almost every city famous in biblical and classical history. Then commenced a decline; and when its terrible Janizaries were a source of danger instead of defense, when its own Sultan was compelled to destroy them in 1826 for the protection of his empire, it was only a helpless mass in the throes of dissolution.

But Turkey as a living and advancing power was less alarming to Europe than Turkey as a perishing one. Lying at the gateway between the East and the West, it occupied the most commanding strategic position in Europe. If that position were held by a living instead of a dying power, that power would be master of the Continent. No one state would ever be permitted by the rest to reach such an ascendency; and the next alternative of a division of the territory after the manner of Poland, was fraught with almost as much danger. The only hope for the peace of Europe was to keep in its integrity this crumbling wreck of a wicked, crime-stained old empire. Such was the policy now inaugurated by Russia, Great Britain, Austria, and Prussia; and such in brief is the "Eastern Question," which for more than half a century has overshadowed all others in European diplomacy, and more than any other has strained the conscience and the moral sense of Christian nations. We wish we might say that one nation had been able to resist this invitation to a moral turpitude masked by diplomatic subterfuges. But there is not one.

Although the question of the balance of power was of importance to all, it was England and Russia to whom the interests involved in the Eastern Question were most vital. Every year which made England's Indian Empire a more important possession also increased the necessity for her having free access to it; while Russian policy more and more revolved about an actual and a potential empire in the East. So just because they were natural enemies they became allies, each desiring to tie the other's hands by the principle of Ottoman integrity.

But daily and noiselessly the Russian outposts crept toward the East; first into Persia, then stretching out the left hand toward Khiva, pressing on through Bokhara into Chinese territory; and then, with a prescience of coming events which should make Western Europe tremble before such a subtle instinct for power, Russia obtained from the Chinese Emperor the privilege of establishing at Canton a school of instruction where Russian youths—prohibited from attending European universities—might learn the Chinese language and become familiarized with Chinese methods! But this was the sort of instinct that impels a glacier to creep surely toward a lower level. Not content with owning half of Europe and all of Northern Asia, the Russian glacier was moving noiselessly,—as all things must,—on the line of least resistance, toward the East.

The Emperor Nicholas, who comprehended so well the secret of imperial expansion, and so little understood the expanding qualities within his empire, was an impressive object to look upon. With his colossal stature and his imposing presence, always tightly buttoned in his uniform, he carried with him an air of majesty never to be forgotten if once it was seen. But while he supposed he was extinguishing the living forces and arresting the advancing power of mind in his empire, a new world was maturing beneath the smooth hard surface he had created. The Russian intellect, in spite of all, was blossoming from seed scattered long before his time. There were historians, and poets, and romanticists, and classicists, just as in the rest of Europe. There were the conservative writers who felt contempt for the West, and for the new, and who believed Russia was as much better before Ivan III. than after, as Ivan the Great was superior to Peter the Great; and there were Pushkin and Gogol, and Koltsof and Turguenief, whom they hated, because their voice was the voice of the New Russia. Turguenief, who with smothered sense of Russia's oppression was then girding himself for his battle with serfdom, says: "My proof used to come back to me from the censor half erased, and stained with red ink like blood. Ah! they were painful times!" But in spite of all, Russian genius was spreading its wings, and perhaps from this very repression was to come that passionate intensity which makes it so great.

CHAPTER XXII.1848 IN EUROPE— CRIMEAN WAR.

The Revolution of 1831 was only the mild precursor of the one which shook Europe to its foundations in 1848. It had centers wherever there were patriots and aching hearts. In Paris, Louis Philippe had fled at the sound of the word Republic, and when in Paris workmen were waving the national banner of Poland, with awakened hope, even that land was quivering with excitement. In Vienna the Emperor Ferdinand, unable to meet the storm, abdicated in favor of his young nephew, Francis Joseph. Hungary, obedient to the voice of her great patriot, Louis Kossuth, in April, 1849, declared itself free and independent. It was the Hungarians who had offered the most encouragement and sympathy to the Poles in 1831; so Nicholas determined to make them feel the weight of his hand. Upon the pretext that thousands of Polish exiles—his subjects—were in the ranks of the insurgents, a Russian army marched into Hungary. By the following August the revolution was over—thousands of Hungarian patriots had died for naught, thousands more had fled to Turkey, and still other thousands were suffering from Austrian vengeance administered by the terrible General Haynau. Francis Joseph, that gentle and benign sovereign, who sits today upon the throne at Vienna, subjected Hungary to more cruelties than had been inflicted by Nicholas in Poland. Not only were the germs of nationality destroyed—the Constitution and the Diet abolished, the national language, church, and institutions effaced; but revolting cruelties and executions continued for years. Kossuth, who with a few other leaders, was an exile and a prisoner in Asia Minor, was freed by the intervention of European sentiment in 1851. The United States government then sent a frigate and conveyed him and his friends to America, where the great Hungarian thrilled the people by the magic of his eloquence in their own language, which he had mastered during his imprisonment by means of a Bible and a dictionary.

It was to Russia that Austria was indebted for a result so satisfactory. The Emperor Nicholas returned to St. Petersburg, feeling that he had earned the everlasting gratitude of the young ruler Francis Joseph, little suspecting that he was before long to say of him that "his ingratitude astonished Europe."

There can be no doubt that the Emperor Nicholas, while he was, in common with the other powers, professing to desire the preservation of Ottoman integrity, had secretly resolved not to leave the Eastern Question to posterity, but to crown his own reign by its solution in a way favorable to Russia. His position was a very strong one. By the Treaty of 1841 his headship as protector of Eastern Christendom had been acknowledged. Austria was now bound to him irrevocably by the tie of gratitude, and Prussia by close family ties and by sympathy. It was only necessary to win over England. In 1853, in a series of private, informal interviews with the English ambassador, he disclosed his plan that there should be a confidential understanding between him and Her Majesty's government. He said in substance: "England and Russia must be friends. Never was the necessity greater. If we agree, I have no solicitude about Europe. What others think is really of small consequence. I am as desirous as you for the continued existence of the Turkish Empire. But we have on our hands a sick man—a very sick man: he may suddenly die. Is it not the part of prudence for us to come to an understanding regarding what should be done in case of such a catastrophe? It may as well be understood at once that I should never permit an attempt to reconstruct a Byzantine Empire, and still less should I allow the partition of Turkey into small republics—ready-made asylums for Kossuths and Mazzinis and European revolutionists; and I also tell you very frankly that I should never permit England or any of the Powers to have a foothold in Constantinople. I am willing to bind myself also not to occupy it—except, perhaps, as a guardian. But I should have no objection to your occupying Egypt. I quite understand its importance to your government—and perhaps the island of Candia might suit you. I see no objection to that island becoming also an English possession. I do not ask for a treaty—only an understanding; between gentlemen that is sufficient. I have no desire to increase my empire. It is large enough; but I repeat—the sick man is dying; and if we are taken by surprise, if proper precautions are not taken in advance, circumstances may arise which will make it necessary for me to occupy Constantinople."

It was a bribe, followed by a threat. England coldly declined entering into any stipulations without the concurrence of the other Powers. Her Majesty's government could not be a party to a confidential arrangement from which it was to derive a benefit. The negotiations had failed. Nicholas was deeply incensed and disappointed. He could rely, however, upon Austria and Prussia. He now thought of Louis Napoleon, the new French Emperor, who was looking for recognition in Europe. The English ambassador was coldly received, and for the first time since the abdication of Charles X., the representative of France received a cordial greeting, and was intrusted with a flattering message to the Emperor. But France had not forgotten the retreat from Moscow, nor the presence of Alexander in Paris, nor her attempted ostracism in Europe by Nicholas himself; and, further, although Louis Napoleon was pleased with the overtures made to win his friendship, he was not yet quite sure which cause would best promote his own ends.

Fortunately Russia had a grievance against Turkey. It was a very small one, but it was useful, and led to one of the most exciting crises in the history of Europe. It was a question of the possession of the Holy Shrines at Bethlehem and other places which tradition associates with the birth and death of Jesus Christ; and whether the Latin or the Greek monks had the right to the key of the great door of the Church at Bethlehem, and the right to place a silver star over the grotto where our Saviour was born. The Sultan had failed to carry out his promises in adjusting these disputed points. And all Europe trembled when the great Prince Menschikof, with imposing suite and threatening aspect, appeared at Constantinople, demanding immediate settlement of the dispute. Turkey was paralyzed with fright, until England sent her great diplomatist Lord Stratford de Redcliffe—and France hers, M. de Lacour. No simpler question was ever submitted to more distinguished consideration or was watched with more breathless interest by five sovereigns and their cabinets. In a few days all was settled—the questions of the shrines and of the possession of the key of the great door of the church at Bethlehem were happily adjusted. There were only a few "business details" to arrange, and the episode would be closed. But the trouble was not over. Hidden away among the "business details" was the germ of a great war. The Emperor of Russia "felt obliged to demand guarantees, formal and positive," assuring the security of the Greek Christians in the Sultan's dominions. He had been constituted the Protector of Christianity in the Turkish Empire, and demanded this by virtue of that authority. The Sultan, strengthened now by the presence of the English and French ambassadors, absolutely refused to give such guarantee, appealing to the opinion of the world to sustain him in resisting such a violation of his independence and of his rights. In vain did Lord Stratford exchange notes and conferences with Count Nesselrode and Prince Menschikof and the Grand Vizier and exhaust all the arts and powers of the most skilled diplomacy. In July, 1853, the Russian troops had invaded Turkish territory, and a French and English fleet soon after had crossed the Dardanelles,—no longer closed to the enemies of Russia,—had steamed by Constantinople, and was in the Bosphorus.

Austria joined England and France in a defensive though not an offensive alliance, and Prussia held entirely aloof from the conflict.

Nicholas had failed in all his calculations. In vain had he tried to lure England into a secret compact by the offer of Egypt—in vain had he preserved Hungary to Austria—in vain sought to attach Prussia to himself by acts of friendship; and his Nemesis was pursuing him, avenging a long series of affronts to France. Unsupported by a single nation, he was at war with three; and after a brilliant reign of twenty-eight years unchecked by a single misfortune, he was about to die, leaving to his empire the legacy of a disastrous war, which was to end in defeat and humiliation.

But a strange thing had happened. For a thousand years Europe had been trying to drive Mohammedanism out of the continent. No sacrifice had been considered too great if it would help to rid Christendom of that great iniquity. Now the Turkish Empire,—the spiritual heir and center of this old enemy,—no less vicious—no less an offense to the instincts of Christendom than before, was on the brink of extermination. It would have been a surprise to Richard the lion-hearted, and to Louis IX. the saint, if they could have foreseen what England and France would do eight hundred years later when such a crisis arrived! While the Sultan in the name of the Prophet was appealing to all the passions of a mad fanaticism to arise and "drive out the foreign infidels who were assailing their holy faith"—there was in England an enthusiasm for his defense as splendid as if the cause were a righteous one.

It is not a simple thing to carry a bark deeply loaded with treasure safely through swift and tortuous currents. England was loaded to the water's edge with treasure. Her hope was in that sunken wreck of an empire which fate had moored at the gateway leading to her Eastern dominions, and what she most feared in this world was its removal. As a matter of state policy, she may have followed the only course which was open to her; but viewed from a loftier standpoint, it was a compromise with unrighteousness when she joined Hands with the "Great Assassin" and poured out the blood of her sons to keep him unharmed. For fifty years that compromise has embarrassed her policy, and still continues to soil her fair name. In the War of the Crimea, England, no less than Russia, was fighting, not for the avowed, but unavowed object. But frankness is not one of the virtues required by diplomacy, so perhaps of that we have no right to complain.

On the 4th of January, 1854, the allied fleets entered the Black Sea. The Emperor Nicholas, from his palace in St. Petersburg, watched the progress of events. He saw Menschikof vainly measuring swords with Lord Raglan at Odessa (April 22); then the overwhelming defeat at the Alma (September 20); then the sinking of the Russian fleet to protect Sebastopol, about which the battle was to rage until the end of the war. He saw the invincible courage of his foe in that immortal act of valor, the cavalry charge at Balaklava (November 5), in obedience to an order wise when it was given, but useless and fatal when it was received—of which someone made the oft-repeated criticism—"C'est magnifique—mais ce n'est pas la guerre." And then he saw the power to endure during that awful winter, when the elements and official mismanagement were fighting for him, and when more English troops were perishing from cold and neglect than had been killed by Russian shot and shell.

But the immense superiority of the armies of the allies could not be doubted. His troops, vanquished at every point, were hopelessly beleagured in Sebastopol. The majesty of his empire was on every side insulted, his ports in every sea blockaded. Never before had he tasted the bitterness of defeat and humiliation. Europe had bowed down before him as the Agamemnon among Kings. He had saved Austria; had protected Prussia; he had made France feel the weight of his august displeasure. Wherever autocracy had been insulted, there he had been its champion and striven to be its restorer. But ever since 1848 there had been something in the air unsuited to his methods. He was the incarnation of an old principle in a new world. It was time for him to depart. His day had been a long and splendid one, but it was passing amid clouds and darkness.

A successful autocrat is quite a different person from an unsuccessful one. Nicholas had been seen in the shining light of invincibility. But a sudden and terrible awakening had come. The nation, stung by repeated defeats, was angry. A flood of anonymous literature was scattered broadcast, arraigning the Emperor—the administration—the ministers—the diplomats—the generals. "Slaves, arise!" said one, "and stand erect before the despot. We have been kept long enough in serfage to the successors of Tatar Khans."

The Tsar grew gloomy and silent. "My successor," he said, "may do what he likes. I cannot change." When he saw Austria at last actually in alliance with his enemies he was sorely shaken. But it was the voice of bitter reproach and hatred from his hitherto silent people which shook his iron will and broke his heart. He no longer desired to live. While suffering from an influenza he insisted upon going out in the intense cold without his greatcoat and reviewing his guards. Five days later he dictated the dispatch which was sent to every city in Russia: "The Emperor is dying."

CHAPTER XXIII.LIBERALISM— EMANCIPATION OF SERFS

When his life and the hard-earned conquests of centuries were together slipping away, the dying Emperor said to his son: "All my care has been to leave Russia safe without and prosperous within. But you see how it is. I am dying, and I leave you a burden which will be hard to bear." Alexander II., the young man upon whom fell these responsibilities, was thirty-seven years old. His mother was Princess Charlotte of Prussia, sister of the late Emperor William, who succeeded to the throne of Prussia, left vacant by his brother in 1861.

His first words to his people were a passionate justification of his father,—"of blessed memory,"—his aims and purposes, and a solemn declaration that he should remain true to his line of conduct, which "God and history would vindicate." It was a man of ordinary flesh and blood promising to act like a man of steel. His own nature and the circumstances of his realm both forbade it. The man on the throne could not help listening attentively to the voice of the people. There must be peace. The country was drained of men and of money. There were not enough peasants left to till the fields. The landed proprietors with their serfs in the ranks were ruined, and had not money with which to pay the taxes, upon which the prosecution of a hopeless war depended. Victor Emmanuel had joined the allies with a Sardinian army; and the French, by a tremendous onslaught, had captured Malakof, the key to the situation in the Crimea. Prince Gortchakof, who had replaced Prince Menschikof, was only able to cover a retreat with a mantle of glory. The end had come.

A treaty of peace was signed March 30, 1856. Russia renounced the claim of an exclusive protectorate over the Turkish provinces, yielded the free navigation of the Danube, left Turkey the Roumanian principalities, and, hardest of all, she lost the control of the Black Sea. Its waters were forbidden to men-of-war of all nations; no arsenals, military or maritime, to exist upon its shores. The fruits of Russian policy since Peter the Great were annihilated, and the work of two centuries of progress was canceled.

Who and what was to blame for these calamities? Why was it that the Russian army could successfully compete with Turks and Asiatics, and not with Europeans? The reason began to be obvious, even to stubborn Russian Conservatives. A nation, in order to compete in war in this age, must have a grasp upon the arts of peace. An army drawn from a civilized nation is a more effective instrument than one drawn from a barbarous one. The time had passed when there might be a few highly educated and subtle intelligences thinking for millions of people in brutish ignorance. The time had arrived when it must be recognized that Russia was not made for a few great and powerful people, for whom the rest, an undistinguishable mass, must toil and suffer. In other words, it must be a nation—and not a dynasty nourished by misery and supported by military force.

Men high in rank no longer flaunted their titles and insignia of office. They shrank from drawing attention to their share of responsibility in the great calamity, and listened almost humbly to the suggestions of liberal leaders, suggestions which, a few months ago, none dared whisper except behind closed doors. A new literature sprang into life, unrebuked, dealing with questions of state policy with a fearless freedom never before dreamed of. Conservative Russia had suddenly vanished under a universal conviction that the hope of their nation was in Liberalism.

The Emperor recalled from Siberia the exiles of the conspiracy of 1825, and also the Polish exiles of 1831. There was an honest effort made to reform the wretched judicial system and to adopt the methods which Western experience had found were the best. The obstructions to European influences were removed, and all joined hands in an effort to devise means of bringing the whole people up to a higher standard of intelligence and well-being. Russia was going to be regenerated. Men, in a rapture of enthusiasm and with tears, embraced each other on the streets. One wrote: "The heart trembles with joy. Russia is like a stranded ship which the captain and the crew are powerless to move; now there is to be a rising tide of national life which will raise and float it."

Such was the prevailing public sentiment in 1861, when Emperor Alexander affixed his name to the measure which was going to make it forever glorious—the emancipation of over twenty-three million human beings from serfdom. It would require another volume to tell even in outline the wrongs and sufferings of this class, upon whom at last rested the prosperity and even the life of the nation, who, absolutely subject to the will of one man, might at his pleasure be conscripted for military service for a term of from thirty to forty years, or at his displeasure might be sent to Siberia to work in the mines for life; and who, in no place or at no time, had protection from any form of cruelty which the greed of the proprietor imposed upon them. Selling the peasants without the land, unsanctioned by law, became sanctioned by custom, until finally its right was recognized by imperial ukases, so that serfdom, which in theory presented a mild exterior, was in practice and in fact a terrible and unmitigated form of human slavery.

Patriarchalism has a benignant sound—it is better than something that is worse! It is a step upward from a darker quagmire of human condition. When Peter the Great, with his terrible broom, swept all the free peasants into the same mass with the unfree serfs, and when he established the empire upon a chain of service to be rendered to the nobility by the peasantry, and then to the state by the nobility, he simply applied to the whole state the Slavonic principle existing in the social unit—the family. And while he was Europeanizing the surface, he was completing a structure of paternalism, which was Asiatic and incompatible with its new garment—an incongruity which in time must bring disorder, and compel radical and difficult reforms.

To remove a foundation stone is a delicate and difficult operation. It needed courage of no ordinary sort to break up this serfdom encrusted with tyrannies. It was a gigantic social experiment, the results of which none could foresee. Alexander's predecessors had thought and talked of it, but had not dared to try it. Now the time was ripe, and the man on the throne had the nerve required for its execution.

The means by which this revolution was effected may be briefly described in a sentence. The Crown purchased from the proprietors the land—with the peasants attached to it, and then bestowed the land upon the peasants with the condition that for forty-five years they should pay to the Crown six per cent. interest upon the amount paid by it for the land. It was the commune or mir which accepted the land and assumed the obligation and the duty of seeing that every individual paid his annual share of rental (or interest money) upon the land within his inclosure, which was supposed to be sufficient for his own maintenance and the payment of the government tax.

These simple people, who had been dreaming of emancipation for years, as a vague promise of relief from sorrow, heard with astonishment that now they were expected to pay for their land! Had it not always belonged to them? The Slavonic idea of ownership of land through labor was the only one of which they could conceive, and it had survived through all the centuries of serfdom, when they were accustomed to say: "We are yours, but the land is ours." Instead of twenty-five million people rejoicing with grateful hearts, there was a ferment of discontent and in some places uprisings—one peasant leader telling ten thousand who rose at his call that the Emancipation Law was a forgery, they were being deceived and not permitted to enjoy what the Tsar, their "Little Father," had intended for their happiness. But considering the intricate difficulties attending such a tremendous change in the social conditions, the emancipation was easily effected and the Russian peasants, by the survival of their old Patriarchal institutions, were at once provided with a complete system of local self-government in which the ancient Slavonic principle was unchanged. At the head of the commune or mir was the elder, a group of communes formed a Volost, and the head of the Volost was responsible for the peace and order of the community. To this was later added the Zemstvo a representative assembly of peasants, for the regulation of local matters.

Such a new reign of clemency awakened hope in Poland that it too might share these benefits. First it was a Constitution such as had been given to Hungary for which they prayed. Then, as Italy was emancipating herself, they grew bolder, and, incited by societies of Polish exiles, all over Europe, demanded more: that they be given independence. Again the hope of a Polo-Lithuanian alliance, and a recovery of the lost Polish provinces in the Ukraine, and the reestablishment of an independent kingdom of Poland, dared to assert itself, and to invite a more complete destruction.

The liberal Russians might have sympathized with the first moderate demand, but when by the last there was an attempt made upon the integrity of Russia, there was but one voice in the empire. So cruel and so vindictive was the punishment of the Poles, by Liberals and Conservatives alike, that Europe at last in 1863 protested. The Polish language and even alphabet were prohibited. Every noble in the land had been involved in this last conspiracy. They were ordered to sell their lands, and all Poles were forbidden to be its purchasers. Nothing of Poland was left which could ever rise again.

CHAPTER XXIV. TURCO-RUSSIAN WAR—TREATY OF BERLIN

Liberalism had received a check. In this outburst of severity, used to repress the free instincts of a once great nation, the temper of the Russian people had undergone a change. The warmth and ardor were chilled. The Emperor's grasp tightened. Some even thought that Finland ought to be Russianized precisely as Poland had been; but convinced of its loyalty, the Grand Principality was spared, and the privileges so graciously bestowed by Alexander the First were confirmed.

While the political reforms had been checked by the Polish insurrection, there was an enormous advance in everything making for material prosperity. Railways and telegraph-wires, and an improved postal service, connected all the great cities in the empire, so that there was rapid and regular communication with each other and all the world. Factories were springing up, mines were working, and trade and production and arts and literature were all throbbing with a new life.

In 1871, at the conclusion of the Franco-Prussian War, the Emperor Alexander saw his uncle William the First crowned Emperor of a United Germany at Paris. The approval and the friendship of Russia at this crisis were essential to the new German Empire as well as to France. Gortchakof, the Russian Chancellor, saw his opportunity. He intimated to the Powers the intention of Russia to resume its privileges in the Black Sea, and after a brief diplomatic correspondence the Powers formally abrogated the neutralization of those waters; and Russia commenced to rebuild her ruined forts and to re-establish her naval power in the South.

There had commenced to exist those close ties between the Russian and other reigning families which have made European diplomacy seem almost like a family affair—although in reality exercising very little influence upon it. Alexander himself was the son of one of these alliances, and had married a German Princess of the house of Hesse. In 1866 his son Alexander married Princess Dagmar, daughter of Christian IX., King of Denmark, and in 1874 he gave his daughter Marie in marriage to Queen Victoria's second son Alfred, Duke of Edinburgh. It was in the following year (1875) that Lord Beaconsfield took advantage of a financial crisis in Turkey, and a financial stringency in Egypt, to purchase of the Khedive his half-interest in the Suez Canal for the sum of $20,000,000, which gave to England the ownership of nearly nine-tenths of that important link in the waterway leading direct to her empire in India.

During all the years since 1856, there was one subject which had been constantly upper-most in the mind of England; and that one subject was the one above all others which her Prime Minister tried to make people forget. It was perfectly well known when one after another of the Balkan states revolted against the Turk—first Herzegovina, then Montenegro, then Bosnia—that they were suffering the cruelest oppression, and that not one of the Sultan's promises made to the Powers in 1856 had been kept. But in 1876 no one could any longer feign ignorance. An insignificant outbreak in Bulgaria took place. In answer to a telegram sent to Constantinople a body of improvised militia, called Bashi-Bazuks, was sent to manage the affair after its own fashion. The burning of seventy villages; the massacre of fifteen thousand—some say forty thousand—people, chiefly women and children, with attendant details too revolting to narrate; the subsequent exposure of Bulgarian maidens for sale at Philippopolis—all this at last secured attention. Pamphlets, newspaper articles, speeches, gave voice to the horror of the English people. Lord Stratford de Redcliffe, Gladstone, John Bright, Carlyle, Freeman, made powerful arraignments of the government which was the supporter and made England the accomplice of Turkey in this crime.

However much we may suspect the sincerity of Russia's solicitude regarding her co-religionists in the East, it must be admitted that the preservation of her Faith has always been treated—long before the existence of the Eastern Question—as the most vital in her policy. In every alliance, every negotiation, every treaty, it was the one thing that never was compromised; and Greek Christianity certainly holds a closer and more mystic relation to the government of Russia than the Catholic or Protestant faiths do to those of other lands.

Russia girded herself to do what the best sentiment in England had in vain demanded. She declared war against Turkey in support of the oppressed provinces of Servia, Herzegovina, and Montenegro. In the month of April, 1877, the Russian army crossed the frontier. Then came the capture of Nikopolis, the repulse at Plevna, the battle of Shipka Pass, another and successful battle of Plevna, the storming of Kars, and then, the Balkans passed,—an advance upon Constantinople. On the 29th of January the last shot was fired. The Ottoman Empire had been shaken into submission, and was absolutely at the mercy of the Tsar, who dictated the following terms: The erection of Bulgaria into an autonomous tributary principality, with a native Christian government; the independence of Montenegro, Roumania, and Servia; a partial autonomy in Bosnia and Herzegovina, besides a strip of territory upon the Danube and a large war indemnity for Russia. Such were the terms of the Treaty of San Stefano, signed in March, 1878. To the undiplomatic mind this seems a happy conclusion of a vexed question. The Balkan states were independent—or partially so; and the Ottoman Empire, although so shorn and shaken as to be innocuous, still remained as a dismantled wreck to block the passage to the East.

But to Beaconsfield and Bismarck and Andrassy, and the other plenipotentiaries who hastened to Berlin in June for conference, it was a very indiscreet proceeding, and must all be done over. Gortchakof was compelled to relinquish the advantages gained by Russia. Bulgaria was cut into three pieces, one of which was handed to the Sultan, another made tributary to him, the third to be autonomous under certain restrictions. Montenegro and Servia were recognized as independent, Bosnia and Herzegovina were given to Austria; Bessarabia, lost by the results of the Crimean War, was now returned to Russia, together with territory about and adjacent to Kars. Most important of all—the Turkish Empire was revitalized and restored to a position of stability and independence by the friendly Powers!

So by the Treaty of Berlin England had acquired the island of Cyprus, and had compelled Russia, after immense sacrifice of blood and treasure, to relinquish her own gains and to subscribe to the line of policy which she desired. A costly and victorious war had been nullified by a single diplomatic battle at Berlin.

The pride of Russia was deeply wounded. It was openly said that the Congress was an outrage upon Russian sensibilities—that "Russian diplomacy was more destructive than Nihilism."

Emperor Alexander had reached the meridian of his popularity in those days of promised reforms, before the Polish insurrection came to chill the currents of his soul. For a long time the people would not believe he really intended to disappoint their hope; but when one reform after another was recalled, when one severe measure after another was enacted, and when he surrounded himself with conservative advisers and influences, it was at last recognized that the single beneficent act history would have to record in this reign would be that one act of 1861. And now his prestige was dimmed and his popularity still more diminished by such a signal diplomatic defeat at Berlin.

CHAPTER XXV. ALEXANDER II. ASSASSINATED—NIHILISM

The emancipation had been a disappointment to its promoters and to the serfs themselves. It was an appalling fact that year after year the death-rate had alarmingly increased, and its cause was—starvation. In lands the richest in the world, tilled by a people with a passion for agriculture, there was not enough bread! The reasons for this are too complex to be stated here, but a few may have brief mention. The allotment of land bestowed upon each liberated serf was too small to enable him to live and to pay his taxes, unless the harvests were always good and he was always employed. He need not live, but his taxes must be paid. It required three days' work out of each week to do that; and if he had not the money when the dreaded day arrived, the tax-collector might sell his corn, his cattle, his farming implements, and his house. But reducing whole communities to beggary was not wise, so a better way was discovered, and one which entailed no disastrous economic results. He was flogged. The time selected for this settling of accounts was when the busy season was over; and Stepniak tells us it was not an unusual thing for more than one thousand peasants in the winter—in a single commune—to be seen awaiting their turn to have their taxes "flogged out." Of course, before this was endured all means had been exhausted for raising the required amount. Usury, that surest road to ruin, and the one offering the least resistance, was the one ordinarily followed. Thus was created that destructive class called Koulaks, or Mir-eaters, who, while they fattened upon the necessities of the peasantry, also demoralized the state by creating a wealthy and powerful class whom it would not do to offend, and whose abominable and nefarious interests must not be interfered with.

Then another sort of bondage was discovered, one very nearly approaching to serfdom. Wealthy proprietors would make loans to distressed communes or to individuals, the interest of the money to be paid by the peasants in a stipulated number of days' work every week until the original amount was returned. Sometimes, by a clause in the contract increasing the amount in case of failure to pay at a certain time, the original debt, together with the accruing interest, would be four or five times doubled. And if, as was probable, the principal never was returned, the peasant worked on year after year gratuitously, in the helpless, hopeless bondage of debt. Nor were these the worst of their miseries, for there were the Tchinovniks—or government officials—who could mete out any punishment they pleased, could order a whole community to be flogged, or at any moment invoke the aid of a military force or even lend it to private individuals for the subjugation of refractory peasants.

And this was what they had been waiting and hoping for, for two centuries and a half! But with touching loyalty not one of them thought of blaming the Tsar. Their "Little Father," if he only knew about it, would make everything right. It was the nobility, the wicked nobility, that had brought all this misery upon them and cheated them out of their happiness! They hated the nobility for stealing from them their freedom and their land; and the nobility hated them for not being prosperous and happy, and for bringing famine and misery into the state, which had been so kind and had emancipated them.

As these conditions became year after year more aggravated acute minds in Russia were employed in trying to solve the great social problems they presented. In a land in which the associative principle was indigenous, Socialism was a natural and inevitable growth. Then, exasperated by the increasing miseries of the peasantry, maddened by the sufferings of political exiles in Siberia, there came into existence that word of dire significance in Russia—Nihilism, and following quickly upon that, its logical sequence—Anarchism, which, if it could, would destroy all the fruits of civilization.

It was Turguenief who first applied the ancient term "Nihilist" to a certain class of radical thinkers in Russia, whose theory of society, like that of the eighteenth-century philosophers in France, was based upon a negation of the principle of authority. All institutions, social and political, however disguised, were tyrannies, and must go. In the newly awakened Russian mind, this first assumed the mild form of a demand for the removal of legislative tyranny, by a system of gradual reforms. This had failed—now the demand had become a mandate. The people must have relief. The Tsar was the one person who could bestow it, and if he would not do so voluntarily, he must be compelled to grant it. No one man had the right to wreck the happiness of millions of human beings. If the authority was centralized, so was the responsibility. Alexander's entire reign had been a curse—and emancipation was a delusion and a lie. He must yield or perish. This vicious and degenerate organization had its center in a highly educated middle class, where men with nineteenth-century intelligence and aspirations were in frenzied revolt against methods suited to the time of the Khans. The inspiring motive was not love of the people, but hatred of their oppressors. Appeals to the peasantry brought small response, but the movement was eagerly joined by men and women from the highest ranks in Russia.

Secret societies and organizations were everywhere at work, recruited by misguided enthusiasts, and by human suffering from all classes. Wherever there were hearts bruised and bleeding from official cruelty, in whatever ranks, there the terrible propaganda found sympathizers, if not a home; men—and still more, women—from the highest families in the nobility secretly pledging themselves to the movement, until Russian society was honeycombed with conspiracy extending even to the household of the Tsar. Proclamations were secretly issued calling upon the peasantry to arise. In spite of the vigilance of the police, similar invitations to all the Russian people were posted in conspicuous places—"We are tired of famine, tired of having our sons perish upon the gallows, in the mines, or in exile. Russia demands liberty; and if she cannot have liberty—she will have vengeance!"

Such was the tenor of the threats which made the life of Emperor Alexander a miserable one after 1870. He had done what not one of his predecessors had been willing to do. He had, in the face of the bitterest opposition, bestowed the gift of freedom upon 23,000,000 human beings. In his heart he believed he deserved the good-will and the gratitude of his subjects. How gladly would he have ruled over a happy empire! But what could he do? He had absolute power to make his people miserable—but none to make them happy. It was not his fault that he occupied a throne which could only be made secure by a policy of stern repression. It was not his fault that he ruled through a system so elementary, so crude, so utterly inadequate, that to administer justice was an impossibility. Nor was it his fault that he had inherited autocratic instincts from a long line of ancestors. In other words, it was not his fault that he was the Tsar of Russia!

The grim shadow of assassination pursued him wherever he went. In 1879 the imperial train was destroyed by mines placed beneath the tracks. In 1880 the imperial apartments in "the Winterhof" were partially wrecked by similar means. Seventeen men marched stolidly to the gallows, regretting nothing except the failure of their crime; and hundreds more who were implicated in the plot were sent into perpetual exile in Siberia. The hand never relaxed—nor was the Constitution demanded by these atrocious means granted.

On the 13th of March, 1881, while the Emperor was driving, a bomb was thrown beneath his carriage. He stepped out of the wreck unhurt. Then as he approached the assassin, who had been seized by the police, another was thrown. Alexander fell to the ground, exclaiming, "Help me!" Terribly mutilated, but conscious, the dying Emperor was carried into his palace, and there in a few hours he expired.

In the splendid obsequies of the Tsar, nothing was more touching than the placing of a wreath upon his bier by a deputation of peasants. It can be best described in their own words. The Emperor was lying in the Cathedral wrapped in a robe of ermine, beneath a canopy of gold and silver cloth lined with ermine. "At last we were inside the church," says the narrative. "We all dropped on our knees and sobbed, our tears flowing like a stream. Oh, what grief! We rose from our knees, again we knelt, and again we sobbed. This did we three times, our hearts breaking beside the coffin of our benefactor. There are no words to express it. And what honor was done us! The General took our wreath, and placed it straightway upon the breast of our Little Father. Our peasants' wreath laid on his heart, his martyr breast—as we were in all his life nearest to his heart! Seeing this we burst again into tears. Then the General let us kiss his hand—and there he lay, our Tsar-martyr, with a calm, loving expression on his face—as if he, our Little Father, had fallen asleep."

If anything had been needed to make the name Nihilism forever odious, it was this deed. If anything were required to reveal the bald wickedness of the creed of Nihilism, it was supplied by this aimless sacrifice of the one sovereign who had bestowed a colossal reform upon Russia. They had killed him, and had then marched unflinchingly to the gallows—and that was all—leaving others bound by solemn oaths to bring the same fate upon his successor. The whole energy of the organization was centered in secreting dynamite, awaiting a favorable moment for its explosion, then dying like martyrs, leaving others pledged to repeat the same horror—and so ad infinitum. In their detestation of one crime they committed a worse one. They conspired against the life of civilization—as if it were not better to be ruled by despots than assassins, as if a bad government were not better than none!

The existence of Nihilism may be explained, though not extenuated. Can anyone estimate the effect upon a single human being to have known that a father, brother, son, sister, or wife has perished under the knout? Could such a person ever again be capable of reasoning calmly or sanely upon "political reforms"? If there were any slumbering tiger-instincts in this half-Asiatic people, was not this enough to awaken them? There were many who had suffered this, and there were thousands more who at that very time had friends, lovers, relatives, those dearer to them than life, who were enduring day by day the tortures of exile, subject to the brutal punishments of irresponsible officials. It was this which had converted hundreds of the nobility into conspirators—this which had made Sophia Perovskaya, the daughter of one of the highest officials in the land, give the signal for the murder of the Emperor, and then, scorning mercy, insist that she should have the privilege of dying upon the gallows with the rest.

But tiger-instincts, whatever their cause, must be extinguished. They cannot coexist with civilization. Human society as constituted to-day can recognize no excuse for them. It forbids them—and the Nihilist is the Ishmael of the nineteenth century.

The world was not surprised, and perhaps not even displeased, when Alexander III. showed a dogged determination not to be coerced into reforms by the assassination of his father nor threats of his own. His coronation, long deferred by the tragedy which threatened to attend it, finally took place with great splendor at Moscow in 1883. He then withdrew to his palace at Gatschina, where he remained practically a prisoner. Embittered by the recollection of the fate of his father, who had died in his arms, and haunted by conspiracies for the destruction of himself and his family, he was probably the least happy man in his empire. His every act was a protest against the spirit of reform. The privileges so graciously bestowed upon the Grand Duchy of Finland by Alexander I. were for the first time invaded. Literature and the press were placed under rigorous censorship. The Zemstvo, his father's gift of local self-government to the liberated serfs, was practically withdrawn by placing that body under the control of the nobility.

It was a stern, joyless reign, without one act intended to make glad the hearts of the people. The depressing conditions in which he lived gradually undermined the health of the Emperor. He was carried in dying condition to Livadia, and there, surrounded by his wife and his children, he expired November 1, 1894.

CHAPTER XXVI. FINLAND—HAGUE TRIBUNAL—POLITICAL CONDITIONS

When Nicholas II., the gentle-faced young son of Alexander, came to the throne there were hopes that a new era for Russia was about to commence. There has been nothing yet to justify that hope. The austere policy pursued by his father has not been changed. The recent decree which has brought grief and dismay into Finland is not the act of a liberal sovereign! A forcible Russification of that state has been ordered, and the press in Finland has been prohibited from censuring the ukase which has brought despair to the hearts and homes of the people. The Russian language has been made obligatory in the university of Helsingfors and in the schools, together with other severe measures pointing unmistakably to a purpose of effacing the Finnish nationality—a nationality, too, which has never by disloyalty or insurrection merited the fate of Poland.

But if this has struck a discordant note, the invitation to a Conference of the Nations with a view to a general disarmament has been one of thrilling and unexpected sweetness and harmony. Whether the Peace Congress at The Hague (1899) does or does not arrive at important immediate results, its existence is one of the most significant facts of modern times. It is the first step on the way to that millennial era of universal peace toward which a perfected Christian civilization must eventually lead us, and it remained for an autocratic Tsar of Russia to sound the call and to be the leader in this movement.

At the death-bed of his father, Nicholas was betrothed to a princess of the House of Hesse, whose mother was Princess Alice, daughter of Queen Victoria. Upon her marriage this Anglo-German princess was compelled to make a public renunciation of her own faith, and to accept that of her imperial consort—the orthodox faith of Russia. The personal traits of the Emperor seem so exemplary that, if he fails to meet the heroic needs of the hour, the world is disposed not to reproach him, but rather to feel pity for the young ruler who has had thrust upon him such an insoluble problem. His character recalls somewhat that of his great-uncle Alexander I. We see the same vague aspiration after grand ideals, and the same despotic methods in dealing with things in the concrete. No general amnesty attended his coronation, no act of clemency has been extended to political exiles. Men and women whose hairs have whitened in Siberia have not been recalled—not one thing done to lighten the awful load of anguish in his empire. It may have been unreasonable to have looked for reforms; but certainly it was not too much to expect mercy!

What one man could reform Russia? Who could reform a volcano? There are frightful energies beneath that adamantine surface—energies which have been confined by a rude, imperfectly organized system of force; a chain-work of abuses roughly welded together as occasion required. It is a system created by emergencies,—improvised, not grown,—in which to remove a single abuse endangers the whole. When the imprisoned forces tried to escape at one spot, more force was applied and more bands and more rivets brutally held them down, and were then retained as a necessary part of the whole.

On the surface is absolutism in glittering completeness, and beneath that—chaos. Lying at the bottom of that chaos is the great mass of Slavonic people undeveloped as children—an embryonic civilization—utterly helpless and utterly miserable. In the mass lying above that exists the mind of Russia—through which course streams of unduly developed intelligence in fierce revolt against the omnipresence of misery. And still above that is the shining, enameled surface rivaling that of any other nation in splendor. The Emperor may say with a semblance of truth l'état c'est moi, but although he may combine in himself all the functions, judicial, legislative, and executive, no channels have been supplied, no finely organized system provided for conveying that triple stream to the extremities. The living currents at the top have never reached the mass at the bottom—that despised but necessary soil in which the prosperity of the Empire is rooted. There has been no vital interchange between the separated elements, which have been in contact, but not in union. And Russia is as heterogeneous in condition as it is in elements. It has accepted ready-made the methods of Greek, of Tatar, and of European; but has assimilated none of them; and Russian civilization, with its amazing quality, its bewildering variety of achievement in art, literature, diplomacy, and in every field, is not a natural development, but a monstrosity. The genius intended for a whole people seems to have been crowded into a few narrow channels. Where have men written with such tragic intensity? Where has there been music suggesting such depths of sadness and of human passion? And who has ever told upon canvas the story of the battlefield with such energy and with such thrilling reality, as has Verestchagin?

The youngest among the civilizations, and herself still only partially civilized, Russia is one of the most—if not the most—important factor in the world-problem to-day, and the one with which the future seems most seriously involved. She has only just commenced to draw upon her vast stores of energy; energies which were accumulating during the ages when the other nations were lavishly spending theirs. How will this colossal force be used in the future? Moving silently and irresistibly toward the East, and guided by a subtle and far-reaching policy, who can foresee what will be the end, and what the ultimate destiny of the Empire which had its beginning in a small Slavonic State upon the Dnieper, and which, until a little more than a century ago, was too much of a barbarian to be admitted into the fraternity of European States.

The farthest removed from us in political ideals, Russia has in the various crises in our national life always been America's truest friend. When others apparently nearer have failed us, she has stood steadfastly by us. We can never forget it. Owning a large portion of the earth's surface, rich beyond calculation in all that makes for national wealth and prosperity, with a peasantry the most confiding, the most loyal, the most industrious in the world, with intellectual power and genius in abundant measure, and with pride of race and a patriotism profound and intense, what more does Russia need? Only three things—that cruelty be abandoned; that she be made a homogeneous nation; and that she be permitted to live under a government capable of administering justice to her people. These she must have and do. In the coming century there will be no place for barbarism. There will be something in the air which will make it impossible that a great part of a frozen continent shall be dedicated to the use of suffering human beings, kept there by the will of one man. There will be something in the air which will forbid cruelty and compel mercy and justice, and which will make men or nations feign those virtues if they have them not.

The antagonism between England and Russia has a deeper significance than appears on the surface. It is not the Eastern question, not the control of Constantinople, not the obtaining of concessions from China which is at stake. It is the question which of two principles shall prevail. The one represented by a despotism in which the people have no part, or the one represented by a system of government through which the will of the people freely acts. There can be but one result in such a conflict, one answer to such a question. The eternal purposes are writ too large in the past to mistake them. And it is the ardent hope of America that Russia—that Empire which has so generously accorded us her friendship in our times of peril—may not by cataclysm from within, but of her own volition, place herself fully in line with the ideals of an advanced civilization.

SUPPLEMENT TO SHORT HISTORY OF RUSSIA

From Rurik to Nicholas III. the policy of Russia has been determined by its thirst for the sea. Every great struggle in the life of this colossal land-locked empire has had for its ultimate object the opening of a door to the ocean, from which nature has ingeniously excluded it. In the first centuries of its existence Rurik and his descendants were incessantly hurling themselves against the door leading to the Mediterranean. But the door would not yield. Then Ivan IV. and his descendants, with no greater success, hammered at the door leading to the West. The thirst growing with defeat became a national instinct. When Peter the Great first looked out upon the sea, at Archangel, and when he created that miniature navy upon the Black Sea, and when he dragged his capital from "Holy Moscow" to the banks of the Neva, planting it upon that submerged tract, he was impelled by the same instinct which is to-day making history in the Far East.

It was in 1582 that Yermak, the Cossack robber and pirate, under sentence of death, won a pardon from Ivan IV. ("the Terrible") in exchange for Siberia—that unknown region stretching across the Continent of Asia to the Pacific. Eight hundred Cossacks under the daring outlaw had sufficed to drive the scattered Asiatic tribes before them and to establish the sovereignty of Yermak, who then gladly exchanged his prize with the "Orthodox Tsar" for his "traitorous head."

It was the tremendous energy of one man, Muraviev, which led to the development of Eastern Siberia. Pathfinder and pioneer in the march across the Asiatic continent, drawing settlers after him as he moved along, he reached the mouth of the Amur river in 1846, and, at last, the empire possessed a naval station upon the Pacific, which was named Nikolaifsk, after the reigning Tsar, Nicholas I.

It was this Tsar, great-grandfather of Nicholas II., who, grimly turning his back upon Western Europe, set the face of Russia toward the East, reversing the direction which has always been the course of empire. What had Russia to gain from alliances in the West? Her future was in the East; and he intended to drive back the tide of Europeanism which his predecessors had so industriously invited. Russian youths were prohibited from being educated in Western universities, and at the same time there was established at Canton a school of instruction where they might learn the Chinese language and the methods and spirit of Chinese civilization. It was a determined purpose to Orientalize his empire. And violating all the traditions of history, the flight of the Russian Eagle from that moment was toward the rising, not the setting sun.

Muraviev, now Governor of the Eastern Provinces of Siberia, was empowered to negotiate a treaty with China to determine the rights of the two nations upon the river Amur, which separated Manchuria, the northernmost province of China, from Russian Siberia. The treaty, which was concluded in 1858, conceded the left bank of this river to Russia.

Nikolaifsk, a great part of the year sealed up with ice, was only a stepping-stone for the next advance southward. From the mouth of the Amur to the frontier of Korea there was a strip of territory lying between the sea on the east and the Ussuri river on the west, which to the Russian mind, at that time, seemed an ideal possession. How it was accomplished it is needless to say; but China reluctantly agreed that there should be for a time a joint occupation of this strip, and, in 1859, needing Russia's friendship, it was unconditionally bestowed. The "Ussuri Region" was now transformed into the "Maritime Provinces of Siberia," and the Russian Empire, by the stroke of a pen, had moved ten degrees toward the south. Vladivostok, at the southern extremity of the new province, was founded in 1860, and in 1872 made chief naval station on the eastern coast, in place of Nikolaifsk.

But the prize obtained after such expenditure of effort and diplomacy was far from satisfactory. Of what use was a naval station which was not only ice-bound half the year but from which, even when ice-free, it was impossible for ships to reach the open sea except by passing through narrow gateways controlled by Japan? How to overcome these obstacles, how to circumvent nature in her persistent effort to imprison her—this was the problem set for Russian diplomacy to solve.

The eastern slice of Manchuria, which now had become the "Maritime Province of Siberia," was a pleasant morsel, six hundred miles long. But there was a still more desired strip lying in the sun south of it—a peninsula jutting out into the sea, the extreme southern end of which (Port Arthur) was ideally situated for strategic purposes, commanding as it does the Gulf of Pechili, the Gulf of Liao-Tung and the Yellow Sea. Who could tell what might happen? China was in an unstable condition. Her integrity was threatened. England, France and Germany, quickly following Russia's lead in the Ussuri strip, had already wrung privileges from her. Circumstances might any day justify Russia's occupation of the entire peninsula. She could afford to wait. And while she waited she was not idle.

The post-road across Asia was no longer adequate for the larger plans developing in the East; so the construction of a railway was planned to span the distance between Moscow and Vladivostok. At a point beyond Lake Baikal the river Amur makes a sudden detour, sweeping far toward the north before it again descends, thus enclosing a large bit of Manchuria in a form not unlike the State of Michigan. Many miles of the projected road might be saved by crossing the diameter of this semi-circle and moving in a straight line to Vladivostok, across Chinese territory. It did not seem wise at this time to ask such a privilege, the patience of China being already strained by the matter of the Ussuri strip, that much-harassed country being also suspicious of the railroad itself. So with consummate tact Russia proceeded to build the road from the two extremities, leaving this gap to be adjusted by time and circumstances. She had not to wait long. In 1894 an unexpected event altered the whole face of the problem. War was declared between China and Japan.

The three Oriental nations involved in this dispute—China, Japan and Korea—offer three distinct and strongly contrasting types coming out of the mysterious region the world used to know by the comprehensive name of Cathay. When we read of 160,000 Japanese soldiers in the year 1600 tramping across Korea for the purpose of conquering their great neighbor China, it has a familiar sound! But China was not conquered by Japan in 1600, and remained the dominant power in the East, as she had been since she struggled out of the Mongol yoke which, in common with Russia, Kublai-Khan imposed upon her in 1260.

At the time of this Mongol invasion, the Manchus, a nomadic tribe, gathered up their portable tents and fled into a province lying beyond the Great Wall, permanently occupying the region now called Manchuria. Remote and obscure, the Manchus were almost unknown to the Chinese until the year 1580, when Tai-Tsu, a remarkable man and born leader, on account of grievances suffered by his tribe, organized a revolt against China and made a victorious assault upon his powerful Suzerain. Upon his death, in 1626, his victories were continued by his son, who overthrew the reigning dynasty and was proclaimed Emperor of China. And that wretched youth who is to-day obscured and dominated by the powerful Empress Dowager at Pekin is the lineal descendant of Tai-Tsu and the last representative of the Manchurian Dynasty, which has ruled China for nearly four centuries.

The Manchus had not much in the way of civilization to impose upon the people they had conquered. But such as they had they brought with them; and the shaven forehead and the queue, so precious to the Chinese, are Manchurian exotics. Mukden, the capital of Manchuria, became the "Sacred City," where Manchurian Emperors at death were laid beside Tai-Tsu. Wealthy mandarins built residences there. It became splendid and, next only to Pekin, was known as the second official city in the empire.

While the world has long been familiar with China and its civilization, Japan and Korea have only recently come out from their Oriental seclusion. In looking into the past of the former, in vain do we seek for any adequate explanation, anything which will reasonably account for that phenomenally endowed race which occupies the centre of the stage to-day; which, knowing absolutely nothing of our civilization forty years ago, has so digested and assimilated its methods and essential principles that it is beating us at our own game.

From its earliest period this country was under a feudal system of government, with the Mikado as its supreme and sacred head. The Divine nature of this being separated him from the temporal affairs of the nation, which were in the hands of the Shogun, who represented the strong arm of the state. Next below the Shogun were the Daimios, the feudal or military chiefs; these in turn being the rulers of bands of military retainers which constituted the aristocratic class, and were called the Samurai.

Shintoism, a form of ancestral worship and sacrifice to dead heroes, which was the primitive cult of Japan, was in 600 A. D. superseded, or rather absorbed, by Buddhism, which for a thousand years has prevailed. And although Shintoism to some extent still lingers, and although Confucianism with its philosophical and abstract principles has always had its followers, still Japanese civilization is the child of Gautama.

The dual sovereignty of the Mikado and the Shogun, like that existing in the Holy Roman Empire, made a great deal of history in Japan. The things representing the real power in a state were in the hands of the Shogun. The Mikado was venerated, but this first servant in the land was feared, the one dwelling in a seclusion so sacred that to look upon him was almost a sacrilege, the other with armies and castles and wealth and the pomp and circumstance which attend the real sovereign. History again repeats itself as we see this Maire du Palais obscuring more and more the titular sovereign, the Mikado, until like Pepin he openly claimed absolute sovereignty, assuming the title of Tycoon.

The people rose against this usurpation. It was while in the throes of this revolution that the United States Government dispatched a few ships under Commodore Perry, in protection of some American citizens in Japan. After this events moved swiftly. In 1854 a treaty with the United States—their first with foreign nations—was signed at Yokohama. Treaties with other nations speedily followed. In 1860 a Japanese embassy arrived at Washington, and similar ones were established in European capitals.

In 1869 the revolution was over. The party of the usurping Tycoon was defeated and the Shogunate abolished. The anti-foreign spirit which was allied with it shared this defeat, and the party desiring to adopt the methods of foreign lands was triumphant. There was a reorganization of the government, with the Mikado as its single and supreme head. The entire feudal structure, with its Daimios and Samurai, was swept away. A representative body was created holding a relation to the Mikado similar to that of the Houses of Parliament to the King of England. The rights of the people were safeguarded. In other words, at a bound, an Oriental feudal and military despotism had become a modern democratic free state. From this moment dates an ascent from obscurity to an advanced type of civilization, accomplished with a swiftness without a parallel in the history of nations.

Japanese youths, silent, intent, studious, were in European and American universities, colleges, technical schools, learning the arts of war and of peace. When war was declared between China and Japan (1894), the world discovered that they had not studied in vain.

In order to understand the Chino-Japanese war, one must know something of Korea, that, little peninsula jutting out between these two countries, washed by the Yellow Sea on the west and by the Sea of Japan on the east.

In the Koreans we seem to behold the wraith of a something which existed long ago. There are traditions of ancient greatness, the line of their present King stretching proudly back to 1390, and beyond that an indefinite background of splendor and vista of heroic deeds which, we are told, made China and Japan and all the East tremble! But to-day we see a feeble and rather gentle race, eccentric in customs and dress and ideals, with odd rites and ceremonials chiefly intended to placate demoniacal beings to whom they ascribe supreme control over human events. Nothing may be done by the King or his humblest subject without consulting the sorcerers and exorcists, who alone know the propitious moment and place for every important act. With no recognition of a Supreme Being, no sacred books; without temples, or art, or literature, or industries, excepting one or two of a very simple nature, it is extremely difficult for the Western mind to understand what life must mean to this people. That it is a degenerate form of national life which must be either absorbed or effaced seems obvious. And if the life of Korean nationality is prolonged in the future, it will be simply because, like Turkey, it harmlessly holds a strategic point too valuable to be allowed to pass into the hands of any one of the nations which covet it.

And it is also easy to foresee that in the interval existing until its absorption, Korea must remain, also like Turkey, merely the plaything of diplomacy and the battle-ground for rival nations.

Until the year 1876 Korea was really a "Hermit Kingdom," with every current from the outside world carefully excluded. In that year her near neighbor, Japan, made the first rift in the enclosing shell. A treaty was concluded opening Chemulpo, Fusan and Won-San to Japanese trade. The civilizing tide pressed in, and by 1883 the United States, France, England and Germany had all concluded treaties and Korea was open to the outside world.

The government of Korea at this time was simply an organized system of robbery and extortion—wearing not even the mask of justice. The undisguised aim of officialdom was to extort money from the people; and the aim of the high-born Korean youth (or yang-ban) was to pass the royal examination in Chinese classics, which was requisite to make him eligible for official position, and then join the horde of vampires who fed upon the people. At irregular intervals there were revolts, and under the pressure of violent acts temporary relief would be afforded; then things would go on as before.

While such was the perennial condition of political unrest, a rebellion of a different sort broke out at Seoul in 1885—an anti-foreign rebellion—which had for its purpose the expulsion of all the foreign legations. This led to negotiations between China and Japan having an important bearing upon subsequent events. Li Hung Chang, representing China, and Marquis Ito, the Japanese Foreign Minister, held a conference (1885) at Tien-tsin, which resulted in what is known as the "Li-Ito treaty." In view of the disorders existing, it was agreed that their respective governments should hold a joint control in Korea, each having the right to dispatch troops to the peninsula if required. This agreement was later expanded into a joint occupation until reform should be established insuring security and order. These negotiations left Korea as before an independent state, although tributary to China.

The Koreans attributed their calamities to their Queen, a woman of intelligence and craft, who managed to keep her own family in the highest positions and also, by intriguing with China, to thwart Japanese reforms. It soon became apparent that so far from co-operating in these reforms, which were an essential part of the Li-Ito agreement, China intended to make them impossible. The Government at Tokio came to a momentous decision.

In 1894 an outbreak more serious than usual occurred, known as the "Tong-Hak Rebellion." Li Hung Chang promptly sent an army from Tien-tsin for its suppression, another from Japan coming simultaneously.

But the Japanese army poured into Chemulpo in such numbers and with a perfection of equipment suggesting a purpose not mentioned in the Li-Ito agreement! China's protest was met by open defiance, Japan declaring that, as the convention of 1885 had been violated, she should no longer recognize the sovereignty of China in Korea.

War was declared Aug. 1, 1894. The Mikado's Government was not unprepared for this crisis. There were no surprises awaiting the army of little men as they poured into Korea. They knew the measurements of the rivers, the depth of the fords and every minutest detail of the land they intended to invade. Their emissaries in disguise had also been gauging the strength and the weakness of China from Thibet to the sea. They knew her corruption, her crumbling defenses, her antique arms and methods, the absence of all provision for the needs of an army in the field.

With a bewildering suddenness and celerity the plan of the campaign developed. First the control of Korea was secured, then the command of the sea, then the Yalu was crossed; and while one division of the army was pouring into Manchuria, threatening Niu-Chwang and beyond that Mukden, a second division landed at Pitsewo, making a rapid descent upon Port Arthur, the chief stronghold of China, which was captured by assault Nov. 20, 1894.

Wei-Hai-Wei, the next strongly fortified point on the coast of China, south of Port Arthur, of almost equal strategic value, was defended with desperation by sea and by land. But in vain; and, with the capitulation of Wei-Hai-Wei, Feb. 12, 1895, the war was ended.

With the "Sacred City" of Mukden threatened in the north, and Pekin in the south, Japan could name her own terms as the price of peace. First of all she demanded an acknowledgment of the independence of Korea. Then that the island of Formosa and the Manchurian peninsula (Liao-Tung), embracing a coast line from the Korean boundary to Port Arthur, should belong to her.

A severe blow had been dealt to Russia. She saw her entire Eastern policy threatened with failure. The permanent occupation of the Liao-Tung peninsula by Japan meant that she had to deal, not with an effete and waning power which she might threaten and cajole, but with a new and ambitious civilization which had just given proof of surprising ability. After vast expenditure of energy and treasure and diplomacy, access to the sea was further off than ever.

Then came a masterly stroke. Germany and France were induced to co-operate with Russia in driving Japan out of Manchuria, upon the ground that her presence so near to Pekin endangered the Chinese Empire, the independence of Korea and the peace of the Orient. So in the hour of her triumph Japan was to be humiliated; the fruits of her victory snatched from her, precisely as the "Berlin Treaty," in 1879, had torn from Russia the fruits of her Turkish victories! Japan wasted no time in protests, but quietly withdrew and, as it is significantly said, "proceeded to double her army and treble her navy!"

As the protector of Chinese interests Russia was in position to ask a favor; she asked and obtained permission to carry the Siberian railway in a straight line through Manchuria, instead of following the Amur in its great northward sweep. The Japanese word for statesman also means chess-player. Russian diplomatists had played their game well. In serving China, they had incidentally removed the Japanese from a position which blocked their own game, and had at the same time opened a way for their railway across that waiting gap in Northern Manchuria.

Just three years after these events Germany, by way of indemnity for the murder of two missionaries, compelled China to lease to her the province of Shantung. Russia immediately demanded similar privileges in the Liao-Tung peninsula. China, beaten to her knees, could not afford to lose the friendship of the Tsar, and granted the lease; and when permission was asked to have a branch of the Russian railway run from Harbin through the length of this leased territory to Port Arthur, humbly conceded that too.

With wonderful smoothness everything had moved toward the desired end. To be sure, the tenure of the peninsula was only by lease, and in no way different from that of Shantung by

Germany. There was no pretext in sight for garrisoning the dismantled fort at Port Arthur, but the fates had hitherto opened closed doors and might do it again. And so she waited. And while she waited the branch road from Harbin moved swiftly down to Mukden, and on through the Manchurian peninsula, and Port Arthur was in direct line of communication with St. Petersburg.

In 1900 the anti-foreign insurrection known as the "Boxer war" broke out in China. Russia, in common with all the Great Powers (now including Japan), sent troops for the protection of the imperiled legations at Pekin. Nothing could better have served the Government of the Tsar. Russian troops poured into Manchuria, and the new road from Harbin bore the Tsar's soldiers swiftly down to Port Arthur. The fort was garrisoned, and work immediately commenced—probably upon plans already drawn—to make of this coveted spot what Nature seemed to have designed it to be—the Gibraltar of the East.

The Western Powers had not been unobservant of these steady encroachments upon Chinese territory, and while a military occupation of the peninsula was necessary at this time, it was viewed with uneasiness; but none was prepared for what followed. Before peace was actually concluded, Russia approached China with a proposition for her permanent occupancy of—not the peninsula alone, but all of Manchuria. A mystifying proposition when we reflect that Japan was forced out of the southern littoral of Manchuria because her presence there threatened Korea, China, and the peace of the world. Port Arthur was no farther from Pekin and Seoul than it was five years before, and it was much nearer to St. Petersburg! And as Russia had already made surprising bounds from Nikolaifsk to Vladivostok, and from Vladivostok to Port Arthur, she might make still another to one or both of these capitals.

So limp and helpless had China become since the overthrow by Japan and the humiliations following the "Boxer war," and so compliant had she been with Russia's demands, that the United States, Great Britain and Japan, fearful that she would yield, combined to prevent this last concession, which under this pressure was refused, and a pledge demanded for the withdrawal of troops before a fixed date, which pledge Russia gave. At the specified dates, instead of withdrawing her troops from Manchuria, Russia reopened negotiations with China, proposing new conditions. Garrisons were being strengthened instead of withdrawn. Strategic positions were being fortified and barracks built in rushing haste. At the same time Russian infantry and bands of Cossacks were crossing the Yalu to protect Russian sawmills and other industries which had also crept into Korea. And when the Korean Government protested, Russian agents claimed the right to construct railways, erect telegraphs or take any required measures for the protection of Russian settlers in Korea; and every diplomatic attempt to open Manchuria or Korea to foreign trade and residents was opposed by Russia as if it were an attack upon her own individual rights.

Surprising as this was to all the Treaty Powers, it had for Japan the added sting of injustice. She had been ejected from her own territory, fairly won in war, because her presence would endanger the independence of Korea and the peace of the Orient. She now saw Russia in full occupation of this very territory, and the absorption of Korea itself threatened.

And what was the object of all this scheming? Not more land! Certainly a nation owning more than a sixth of the earth's surface could not be hungering for land! And no doubt Russia would long ago gladly have given one-half of Siberia to the sea in exchange for a few good harbors such as existed on the east coast of Korea. It was that ever-existent thirst for access to the ocean which tempted her into tortuous diplomacy, drawing her on and on, like the hand of fate. Manchuria itself would be unavailing unless she could control Korea, which alone possessed the ocean facilities for which she had struggled since the first year of her existence.

In the year 1900 the Trans-Siberian Railway was completed. Its 6,600 miles of rails, if laid in a straight line, would pass one-quarter of the distance around the earth! It had traversed an unexplored continent, creating, as it moved along, homes for the workmen, schools for their technical instruction, churches, hospitals, inns, stores; converting a wilderness, in fact, into a semi-civilization at the rate of a mile a day for nine years! And whereas in the days of the Mongol subjection it required four years for the Grand Princes to go from Moscow to Saraï, near Pekin, to prostrate themselves before the Great Khan, many perishing by the way from fatigue and exposure, the journey from Moscow to Pekin may now be accomplished in two weeks. In perfect good faith Japan commenced her task of reformation in Korea. But the way was obstructed by the large and powerful family of the Queen, who were, in fact, the chief vampires in the kingdom. A few Korean miscreants led by Japanese officials formed a plot to get rid of these people, seize the Government, and then administer the reforms themselves. Forcing their way into the palace Oct. 8, 1895, there was enacted a tragedy similar to the one which recently horrified the world in Servia. While the King was being insulted and dragged about by his hair, the fleeing Queen was stricken down and stabbed, several members of her family sharing the same fate. She, it is said, was then carried, still breathing, to a grove in the park, where, after having kerosene poured over her, she was incinerated. Such was the fate of the intriguing but fascinating Queen of Korea, of whom Count Inouye said: "She has few equals in her country for shrewdness and sagacity, and in the power of conciliating enemies and attaching friends."

The King, a prisoner in his palace, allowed to see or speak with no one, unaware of the death of the Queen (as were all except those engaged in the plot), was compelled to sign odious edicts framed by a cabinet composed of men upon whose hands the blood of his adored wife was scarcely dry. The first of these brought for his signature was a royal decree deposing the Queen, "who for 33 years has dulled our senses, sold offices and titles," etc., etc. "Since she will not give up her wickedness and is hiding and plotting with low fellows, we hereby depose her and degrade her to the lowest rank." The King declared he would have both his hands cut off before he would sign this infamous paper, which did not prevent its appearing with his name attached.

After four months of this torture the wretched man escaped in disguise and found safe asylum in the Russian Legation, where he remained for one year.

One of these reforming edicts signed under compulsion had ordered the immediate abolishment of the Top Knot. The Top Knot was the symbol of nationality and personal dignity. A man without it was less than nothing, and its assumption was the most important event in his life. The ceremony was costly. But what money could be saved from the officials was freely given to the sorcerers and astrologers, who must determine the proper moment and place, and the sacrifices which would be required when their ancestors were informed of the important event which had taken place! Then, when this horn-shaped knot had been covered by a high hat of gauze tied tightly on with ribbons, the Korean arose transformed into a being of dignity and consequence. It was the abolishment of this sacred adornment which brought about a rebellion. Those who did not obey the order were hiding from the officials, while those who did were mobbed and in danger of being killed by the populace.

The King's first act after his escape was to issue a royal proclamation disclaiming with horror the edict degrading and casting infamous reflections upon his beloved Queen. It also rescinded the edicts he had signed under compulsion. It said: "As to the Top Knot, no one shall be forced. Do as you please"; and he continues: "Traitors by their crimes have made trouble. Soldiers, come and protect us! You are our children! You are all pardoned. But when you meet the chief traitors" (naming them) "cut off their heads at once and bring them.

"Soldiers, attend us at the Russian Legation."

Within an hour all were aware of the repeal of the Top Knot decree, and several of the cabinet officers had been beheaded on the streets of Seoul.

Although the Government of the Mikado was innocent of any complicity with this crime, renegade Japanese officials had been leaders in the plot, and Japanese ascendancy had received a severe blow. A point had also been secured by Russia, when the King for one year ruled his kingdom from her legation at Seoul. It is easy to conceive that the distracted man, grateful for protection, did at this time, as is supposed, consent to the purchase of lands and cutting of timber by the Russians on the Yalu, which the following year (1896) expanded into a grant of an extended tract, and became the centre of a large Russian industry in Northern Korea. And it is significant that Admiral Alexieff was one of the prime movers in this project, which to Japan seemed to have a thinly veiled political purpose, and which became, in fact, one of the chief casus belli.

In 1899 the Tsar issued an order for the creation of a city on the Bay of Talien-Wan; and in two years Dalny stood in massive completeness, with docks and wharves and defences which had cost millions of dollars. Millions more had been expended upon Port Arthur, and still more millions upon the railway binding Manchuria to Russia with bands of steel. This did not look like temporary occupation; like pitching her tent for a passing emergency. Still, in the frequent interchange of notes with the powers, there was never an acknowledgment that a permanent occupation was intended. In displeasure at these repeated violations of solemn pledges the Western Powers held aloof; the United States and Great Britain, however, insistently declaring that the "open-door" policy must be maintained, i.e., that all nations must have equal industrial and commercial opportunities in Manchuria and Korea, and also that the integrity of China must be preserved.

In the hope of arriving at a peaceful adjustment of their differences, Japan made a proposition based upon mutual concessions. She would accept the Russian economic status in Manchuria if Russia would recognize hers in Korea.

Russia absolutely refused to admit Japan's right to have anything whatever to say concerning

Manchuria—the land which eight years before was hers by right of conquest, and from which Russia for her own purposes had ejected her. Admiral Alexieff was Viceroy of the Eastern Provinces, and to him the Tsar confided the issues of peace or war. Confident in her enormous weight and military prestige, Russia undoubtedly believed that the Japanese must in the end submit. But after five months of fruitless negotiations the patience of the Government at Tokio was exhausted. On Feb. 8, 1904, the Japanese fleet made a sudden descent upon Port Arthur. This act, so audaciously planned, resulted in the destruction of battle-ships, cruisers, torpedo-boats—nine in all—to which were added the day following two more battle-ships, destroyed at Chemulpo.

There was dismay and grief at St. Petersburg. The Tsar, realizing that he had been misled regarding the chances of peace and also the military strength of the foe, recalled Admiral Alexieff from Port Arthur. Admiral Makaroff, Russia's military hero and ablest commander, succeeded him. Just as his invigorating influence was being felt in awakened energy and courage, there came another disaster more terrible than the first. The Petropavlovsk, flag-ship of the fleet, coming in contact with a submarine mine or boat, was torn to pieces and sank in two minutes, with all on board, including Admiral Makaroff and his entire staff of seventeen officers.

Still benumbed by these crushing blows, the Russians were bewildered by the electrical swiftness with which the campaign developed, moving on lines almost identical with those in the war with China, ten years before. A miracle of discipline and minute perfection in method and detail, the Mikado's army of little men first secured control in Korea, then the command of the sea. Then one army division crossed the Yalu with three converging lines, moving toward Mukden, pressing a retreating army before them. Then, still moving in the grooves of the last war, there was a landing of troops at Pitsewo, threatening Dalny and Port Arthur, the latter already isolated, with railroad and telegraphic lines cut. Seeing the capture of Dalny was imminent, without a pause the Russians mined the harbor, docks and defences which had cost millions of dollars, and the city created by fiat was by fiat doomed to destruction.

Behind this life and death struggle with a foreign foe, another struggle nearer home was being profoundly affected by these unexpected calamities. An unpopular war cannot afford to be an unsuccessful one. This clash with Japan was distinctly the outcome of bureaucratic ambitions and policy. It had not one single issue in which the people who were fighting its battles and bearing its burdens were even remotely interested. And then again—a despotism must not show signs of weakness. Its power lies in the fiction of its invincibility. Liberals and Progressives of all shades, wise and not wise, saw their opportunity. Finns and Poles grew bolder. The air was thick with threats and demands and rumors of revolt.

At this critical moment M. Von Plehve, the leader of the party of reaction, the very incarnation of the spirit of old Russia, of Pobiedonostseff and the Holy Synod, was in power.

In 1903 there had occurred a shocking massacre of Jews at Kishineff. This culmination of a prolonged anti-Semitic agitation was quickly followed by an imperial edict, promising, among other reforms, religious liberty for all. With M. de Witte, the leader of the progressive party, to administer this new policy, a better day seemed to be dawning. But under the benumbing pressure of autocratic influences, and with his characteristic infirmity of purpose, the Tsar almost immediately removed M. de Witte, replacing him with M. Von Plehve, in whose hands the reforming edict became practically inoperative, and in fact all reforms impossible.

On June 15, 1904, General Bobrikov, the recently appointed Russian Governor of Finland, was assassinated by the son of a Finnish Senator within the walls of the Senate. Quickly following this, July 28th, M. Von Plehve was killed on the streets of St. Petersburg by the explosion of a dynamite bomb. The Tsar, recognized the meaning of these events, and quickly appointed Prince Mirski, known by his liberal tendencies, to Von Plehve's place in the Ministry of the Interior. One of the first acts of the new minister was the authorizing of a meeting of all the Presidents of the Zemstvos for consultation over national conditions. When it is recalled that the Zemstvo is a Peasants' Court, that it is a representative assembly of the humblest class in the Empire, and a gift which accompanied emancipation bestowed for their own protection—when this is remembered, we realize the full significance of this act of M. Von Plehve's successor. This first conference of the heads of the Zemstvos, which met at Moscow, Nov., 1904, by permission of Prince Mirski, contained the germ of a representative government. It was an acknowledgment of a principle hitherto denied; a recognition never before made of the right of the people to come together for the purpose of discussing measures of governmental policy.

In the meantime the Japanese, irresistible as fate, were breaking down one after another of the supposed impregnable defences about Port Arthur; climbing over hills of their own dead, fathers, sons, and brothers, in order to do it. Within the beleaguered fort the supply of ammunition was running low, only one-quarter of the defenders were left, and disease was slaying and incapacitating these. Nearer and nearer came the rain of fire. In vain they listened for the booming of Kuropatkin's guns sweeping down from the north. In vain they watched for the smoke of the long-promised Baltic fleet approaching from the south. No rescue came. On the last night of the year, after consultation with his officers, General Stoessel signed the conditions of capitulation to General Nogi. The key to the Russian power in the East was lost. When the new year dawned the Japanese flag floated from the Citadel on the Golden Hill, and the greatest siege of modern times was ended.

On Jan. 1, 1905, General Stoessel wrote to his Imperial Master: "Great Sovereign, pardon us! We have done everything humanly possible. Judge us, but be merciful!" He then goes on to state the conditions which would make further resistance a wanton sacrifice of the lives of those remaining in the garrison.

St. Petersburg was stunned by the receipt of this intelligence; and every day added to its dismay: Oyama, leaving the captured fortress behind him, sweeping the Russians back from Mukden; Kuropatkin sending despairing messages to the Tsar, who, bewildered and trembling before his own subjects at home, was still vibrating between the two widely opposing influences—the spirit of the old despotism, and that of a new age which clamored to be admitted.

Rescript followed quickly upon rescript; one sounding as if written by de Witte, the other as if dictated by Pobiedonostseff; while alarming rumors were coming hourly from Moscow, Finland, Poland, the Crimea, the Caucasus; and the great fabric before which the world had trembled seemed threatened at every vital point.

In the midst of these colossal disasters stood a young man not fashioned for great events—from whom the world and the situation demand a statesmanship as able as Bismarck's, a political ideal as exalted as Washington's, a prompt and judicious dealing with an unprecedented crisis worthy of Peter the Great. And not finding this ample endowment, we call him a weakling. It is difficult for the Anglo-Saxon, fed and nourished for a thousand years upon the principles of political freedom and their application, to realize the strain to which a youth of average ability is subjected when he is called upon to cast aside all the things he has been taught to reverence,—to abandon the ideals he holds most sacred,—to violate all the traditions of his ancestors,—to act in direct opposition to the counsel of his natural advisers; and to do all these things at the dictation of men he has been taught not only to distrust, but to hold in contempt.

Chief among his counsellors is the Procurator Pobiedonostseff, head of the "Holy Synod,"— that evil genius of two reigns, who reminds him of the sacredness of his trust, and his duty to leave his divine heritage to his son unimpaired by impious reforms. Next to him stands Muravieff, the wise and powerful Minister of Justice, creator of modern Siberia, and member of the Court of Arbitration at The Hague, who speaks with authority when he tells him he has not the right to change a political system created by his predecessors; and still nearer than these are the Grand Dukes, a phalanx of uncles and imperial relatives surrounding him with a petrified wall of ancient prejudices. Confronting these imposing representatives of imperial and historic Russia are a few more or less discredited men, like M. de Witte and Prince Mirski, counselling and warning with a freedom which would once have sent them to Siberia, and with a power to which the bewildered Nicholas cannot be indifferent, and to which, perhaps, he would gladly yield were it not for the dominating sentiment about him. Many a man who could face a rain of bullets without a tremor, would quail and turn coward if subjected to the same test before such a cumulative force of opinion.

But this is not a crisis to be settled in the Council-Chamber, nor to be decided by convincing arguments, but by the march of events. And events were not slow in coming.

The assassination of the Grand Duke Sergius, uncle of the Tsar, and the most extreme of the reactionaries at Moscow, of which he was governor, was the most powerful argument yet presented for a change of direction in the Government; and others were near at hand.

The derangement of industrial conditions induced by the war pressed heavily upon the wage-earners; and the agitation upon the surface, the threatened explosions here and there, were only an indication of the misery existing in the deeps below. At all industrial centres there were strikes accompanied by the violence which invariably attends them.

On the morning of Sunday, Jan. 22d, an orderly concourse of workmen, in conformity with a plan already announced, were on their way to the Winter-Palace bearing a petition to the "Little Father," who, if he only knew their wrongs, would see that justice was done them. So they were going to tell him in person of their grievances. The letter of the preceding day ran thus:

"Sovereign. We fear the ministers have not told you the whole truth. Your children, trusting in you, have resolved to come to the Winter Palace tomorrow at 2 P. M. to tell you of their needs.

Appear before us and receive our address of devotion."

Had these 8,000 or 10,000 men been marching to the Winter-Palace with rifles in their hands, or with weapons of any sort indicating a violent purpose, there might have been cause for alarm. But absolutely unarmed, even for their own defence, led by an orthodox priest carrying an icon, these humble petitioners were met by a volley of rapid fire from repeating rifles, were cut down by sabres and trampled by cavalry, until "policing" had become an indiscriminate massacre of innocent people upon the streets, regardless of age or sex. Before midnight the Tsar was miles away at his Palace Tsarskoe-Selo; and there was a new cry heard in St. Petersburg, a cry unfamiliar to Russian ears,—"Down with the Tsar!" Those blood-stains in Nevski Prospect will be long in effacing!

The long-looked-for Baltic fleet, commanded by Admiral Rojestvenski, was detained at the outset of its voyage by an untoward incident, having fired into a fleet of British fishermen, which was mistaken for the enemy in disguise. After being acquitted by a court of inquiry, the Admiral proceeded, his objective point now being changed from Port Arthur to Vladivostock, the next most critical point.

On May 27-28th there occurred one of the most disastrous naval engagements in the annals of war, in the Korean Straits, near Tsushima, where Admiral Togo with sure instinct of the course which would be taken, was lying in wait under the cover of darkness and fog.

Nineteen Russian vessels were destroyed, the Japanese ships sustaining almost no injury. All that remained of the Russian fleet was surrendered to Admiral Togo, and Rojestvenski, desperately wounded, and all of his surviving officers, were prisoners of war in Tokio.

With this climax of Russian disaster the end had come. Although Russia still doggedly refused to acknowledge defeat, and made feint of preparation for reënforcements and future triumphs, the world saw that there must be peace; and that the only existing obstacle was the determination of a proud nation not to be placed in a humiliating position.

The absolute neutrality of the United States enabled President Roosevelt to intervene at this critical moment as no European sovereign could have done. His proposal that there should be a meeting of envoys for the discussion of some peaceable adjustment of their differences was promptly accepted by both nations, and with the hostile armies still facing each other in Manchuria, arrangements were made for the Peace Conference to be held in the United States in August.

The envoys selected for this mission were M. de Witte and Baron Rosen, Ambassador to the United States from Russia, on the one hand, and Baron Komura, Minister of Foreign Affairs in Japan, and Kogaro Takahira, Minister at Washington from that country, on the other. If the appointment of M. de Witte had awakened expectation of a presentation of the Russian cause from the view-point of a progressive leader, the mistake was quickly discovered. M. de Witte, performing a duty intrusted to him by his Imperial master, was quite a different person from de Witte, the exponent of liberal ideas, pleading the cause of an oppressed people before the Tsar; and an adamantine side of his character, quite unexpected, was revealed. The fencing between the two skilled diplomats, de Witte and Komura, afforded a fascinating study in racial methods and characteristics at a high point of development; the impression left being that the intense sincerity of purpose in the Japanese, and the lack of it in the other, was the main point of difference. The Russian argument throughout was upon a perfectly insincere basis. The Russian envoy never once recognized that he represented a defeated nation, steadily maintaining the attitude of a generous foe willing to stop fighting to prevent the shedding of more blood. In striking contrast to this was Baron Komura's calm presentation of his twelve peace proposals, and the sad sincerity with which he tenaciously maintained their justification by the results of the war.

Eight of these proposals, of minor importance, were accepted, while the four of real significance were at once rejected by M. de Witte. These were: the cession of the Island of Saghalien, already partly occupied by the Japanese troops; the interning of all Russian ships lying in Japanese waters; an indemnity of $600,000,000 to reimburse Japan for the cost of the war, and a limitation of the naval power of Russia.

Many times negotiations were on the verge of breaking; at the last of these crises, when the hope of an agreement was actually abandoned and preparations were making for departure, it is said, strong pressure was brought to bear upon Japan by President Roosevelt which led to a modification of the terms—a modification so excessive that deep resentment existed in Tokio, and a satisfaction correspondingly great was experienced in St. Petersburg. Japan withdrew her demands for indemnity and for acquisition of territory in the following way: she saved her adversary from the humiliation of reimbursing her for the cost of the war by offering to sell to Russia the northern half of the island in dispute,—Saghalien,—for two-thirds of the sum she had demanded under the name of indemnity.

The Russo-Japanese treaty of peace, signed at Portsmouth in August, 1905, registers the concession of all the vital points in the demands of the conquering nation. The popular saying, "to the victor belong the spoils," does not hold good in Japan! Twice has she seen the fruits of her splendidly won victories snatched from her by the same hand; and twice has she looked with far-seeing eyes into the future, and quietly submitted. Perhaps she realizes that a time may come when Russia's friendship will be more valuable to her than Saghalien!

The war was over. The march of armies had ceased; but the march of events, accelerated by the great upheaval, moved irresistibly on. Realizing that something must be done to pacify the people, a new and more liberal policy was announced, with de Witte, now Prime Minister, in charge. Russia was to have a National Assembly, a law-making body in which every class would have representation.

This Russian Parliament was to be composed of two bodies: an Upper and a Lower House. The one to be called the "Council of the Empire," the other the "Duma." These were to be convoked and prorogued annually by Imperial Ukase. The President, Vice-President, and one-half the members of the Council of the Empire (consisting of 178 members) were to be appointed by the Tsar; twenty-four more to be elected by the nobility and clergy, a very small number by some designated universities and commercial bodies; each Zemstvo (of which there are fifty-one) being entitled to one representative. The members composing the Duma, or Lower House, were to be elected by the Electoral Colleges, which had in turn been created by the votes of the people in the various provinces of the Empire for that purpose.

The two bodies were to have equal rights in initiating legislation. But a bill must pass both Houses and then receive Imperial Sanction in order to become a law; and failing in this, cannot come up again during the same session. Thus hedged about and thus constituted, it is obvious that a conservative majority was permanently secured and ways provided to block any anti-imperial or revolutionary legislation in the Duma. And when it is added that matters concerning finance and treasonable offences were almost entirely in the hands of the Council, we realize how this gift of political representation to the Russian people had been shorn of its dangers!

The first National Assembly was opened by the Tsar May 10, 1906, with the form and splendor of a court ceremonial. It was a strange spectacle, that solid body of 100 peasants seated on the left of the throne, intently listening to the brief and guarded speech of welcome to the "representatives of the nation, who had come to aid him in making laws for their welfare!" And the first jarring note came when not one of these men joined in the applause which followed.

The first Duma was composed of 450 members. The world was watching this experiment, curious to find out what sort of beings have been dumbly supporting the weight of the Russian Empire. Almost the first act was a surprise. Instead of explosive utterances and intemperate demands, the Duma formally declared Russia to be a Constitutional Monarchy. No anarchistic extravagance could have been so disturbing to autocratic Russia as was this wise moderation, which at the very outset converted Constitutional Bureaucrats into Constitutional Democrats, thus immensely strengthening the people's party at the expense of the Conservatives. The leaders in the Duma knew precisely what they wanted, and how to present their demands with a clearness, a power, and a calm determination for which Russia,—and indeed that greater audience, the world at large,—was quite unprepared. That this seriously alarmed the Imperial party was proved by an immediate strengthening of the defences about the throne by means of a change in what is called the Fundamental Laws. These Fundamental Laws afford a rigid framework, an immovable foundation for the authority of the Emperor and his Cabinet Ministers.

Repairs in the Constitution of the United States have been usually in the direction of increased liberties for the people. The Tsar, on the contrary, aided by his Cabinet and high Government officials, drafted a new edition of the Fundamental Laws suited to a new danger.

The changes made were all designed to build up new defences around the throne, and to intrench more firmly every threatened prerogative. The Tsar was deliberately ranging himself with the bureaucratic party instead of the party of his people; and the hot indignation which followed found expression in bitter and powerful arraignment of the Government, even to the extent of demanding the resignation of the Ministry. What was at first a rift, was becoming an impassable chasm.

If Count Witte had disappointed the Liberals by his lukewarmness and by what they considered an espousal of the conservative cause, he was even less acceptable to the Bureaucrats, to whom he had from the first been an object of aversion—an aversion not abated by his masterly diplomacy at Portsmouth, for which he received only a grudging acknowledgment. Whatever may be the verdict of the future, with its better historic perspective, whether justly or unjustly, Count Witte had lost his hold upon the situation; and the statesman who had been the one heroic figure in Russia was no longer the man of the hour. At all events, his resignation of the head of the Ministry during this obnoxious attempt to nullify the gift of popular representation was significant; and the name of de Witte is not associated with this grave mistake made by the master he has tried to serve.

The reforms insistently demanded by the Duma were as follows:—The responsibility of the Ministry to that body, as the representative of the people; the distribution to the working peasants of the lands held by the Crown and the clergy; a General Amnesty, with the release of all political prisoners; and the abolition of the death penalty.

This was virtually a sweeping demand for the surrender of the autocratic principle, the very principle the Fundamental Laws had just been revised to render more inviolable. The issue was now narrowed down within definite limits. It was a conflict for power, for administrative control, and it was a life-and-death struggle between the Tsar and his people.

Printed reports of the debates were sent broadcast, and for the first time since Russia came into being the peasantry saw things as they really were. They had always attributed their wrongs to the nobility, who, they believed, had cheated them out of their land and their rights under the Emancipation Act. But now it was not the nobility, not the hated Boyars who were cruelly refusing to give them land and liberty, but it was the Little Father, he whom they had always trusted and adored!

It is a critical moment when the last illusion drops from the eyes of a confiding people. The Duma at this moment was engaged in a task of supreme difficulty and responsibility. Millions of people hung upon its words and acts. A group of inexperienced but terribly determined men were facing an equally determined group of well-seasoned officials, veterans in the art of governing. Never was there greater need of calmness and wisdom, and at this very time a wild revolutionary faction was doing its utmost to inflame the passions of a peasantry already maddened with a sense of wrong and betrayal, who in gusts of destructive rage were burning, pillaging, and carrying terror into the remotest parts of the Empire.

Even while the Duma was demanding this larger measure of liberty and of authority over the Ministry, that body had already initiated and put in force new and more vigorous methods of suppression. Under M. Durnovo, Minister of the Interior, a law had been promulgated known as the Law of Reinforced Defense. Under the provisions of this law, high officials, or subordinates designated by them, were clothed with authority to arrest, imprison, and punish with exile or death, without warrant, without accusation, or any judicial procedure whatever.

On July 16, 1906, M. Makaroff, Assistant Secretary of the Interior, appeared personally before the Duma; and in answer to thirty-three interpellations concerning as many specific cases of imprisonment without resort to the courts, frankly replied: "Yes. We have held the persons named in prison for the time mentioned without warrant or accusation; and some of these, and many others, have been exiled to Siberia. But it is a precaution demanded by the situation and the circumstances; a precaution we are authorized to take by the Law of Reinforced Defense."

In October of last year (1905) the world was made glad by a manifesto issued by the Tsar containing these words: "In obedience to our inflexible will, we hereby make it the duty of our Government to give to our beloved people freedom of conscience, freedom of speech, freedom of public assembly, freedom of association, and real inviolability of personal rights." The Tsar had also, with the same solemnity, declared: "No law shall take effect without the sanction of the Duma, which is also to have participation in the control of the officials." Yet, Ministers and Governors General, or subordinates appointed by them, may at their own discretion imprison, exile, or kill in defiance of Imperial command, and find ample protection in the Law of Reinforced Defense!

The free handling of these governmental methods in the Duma, and the immediate world-wide publicity given to these revelations, if allowed to continue, must inevitably destroy the cause of Russian Bureaucracy. There were but two courses open to the Tsar. He must either surrender the autocratic principle, and in good faith carry out his pledges and share his authority with his people, or he must disperse a representative body which flagrantly defied his Imperial will. He chose the latter course.

Five days after the examination of M. Makaroff, on July 21, 1906, the first Russian Parliament was dissolved by Imperial ukase.

The reason assigned for this was that, "instead of applying themselves to the work of productive legislation, they have strayed into a sphere beyond their competence, and have been making comments on the imperfections of the Fundamental Laws, which can only be modified by our Imperial will."

The Tsar at the same time declared his immutable purpose to maintain the institution of Parliament, and named March 5, 1907, as the date of the convening of a new Duma.

A body of 186 Representatives, including the Constitutional and Conservative members of the Duma, immediately reassembled at Viborg in Finland, where, in the few hours before their forcible dispersion by a body of military, they prepared an address to "The Citizens of All Russia." This manifesto was a final word of warning, in which the people were reminded that for seven months, while on the brink of ruin, they are to stand without representation; also reminding them of all that may be done in that time to undermine their hopes, and to obtain a pliable and subservient Parliament, if, indeed, any Parliament at all be convoked at the time promised by the Tsar.

In view of all this they were solemnly abjured not to give "one kopek to the throne, or one soldier to the army," until there exists a popular representative Parliament.

The hand of autocracy is making a final and desperate grasp upon the prerogatives of the Crown. When the end will come, and how it will come, cannot be foretold. But it needs no prophetic power to see what that end will be. The days of autocracy in Russia are numbered. A century may be all too short for the gigantic task of habilitating a Russian people—making the heterogeneous homogeneous, and converting an undeveloped peasantry into a capable citizenship. The problem is unique, and one for which history affords no parallel. In no other modern nation have the life forces been so abnormal in their adjustment. And it is only because of the extraordinary quality of the Russian mind, because of its instinct for political power, and its genius for that instrument of power hitherto known as diplomacy—it is only because of these brilliant mental endowments that this chaotic mass of ethnic barbarism has been made to appear a fitting companion for her sister nations in the family of the Great Powers.

It is vain to expect the young Tsar to set about the task of demolishing the autocratic system created by his predecessors and ancestors. That work is in charge of more august agents. It is perishing by natural process because it is vicious, because it is out of harmony with its environment, and because the maladjusted life forces are moving by eternal laws from the surface to their natural home in the centre. And we may well believe that the fates are preparing a destiny commensurate with the endowments of a great—perhaps the greatest—of the nations of the earth.

Let it not be supposed that it is the moujik, the Russian peasant in sheepskin, with toil-worn hands, who has conducted that brilliant parliamentary battle in the Duma. Certain educational and property qualifications are required for eligibility to membership in that body, which would of necessity exclude that humble class. It is not the emancipated serf, but it is rural Russia which the Duma represented, and the vastness of the area covered by that term is realized when one learns that of the 450 members constituting that body only eighteen were from cities. It is the leaders of this vast rural population, members of ancient princely families or owners of great landed estates, these are the men who are coming out of long oblivion to help rule the destinies of a new Russia. Men like Prince Dolgorouki, some of them from families older than the Romanoffs—such men it is who were the leaders in the Duma. They have been for years studying these problems, and working among the Zemstvos. They are country gentlemen of the old style,—sturdy, practical, imaginative, idealistic, and explosive; powerful in debate, bringing just at the right moment a new element, a new force. Happy is Russia in possessing such a reserve of splendid energy at this time. And if the moujik is not in the forefront of the conflict, he, too, affords a boundless ocean of elementary force—he is the simple barbarian, who will perhaps be needed to replenish with his fresh, uncorrupted blood the Russia of a new generation.

LIST OF PRINCES.

GRAND PRINCES OF KIEV.
Rurik,   862-879
Oleg (Brother of Rurik, Regent),   879-912
Igor (Son of Rurik), 912-945
Olga (Wife of Igor, Regent),   945-964
Sviatoslaf,   964-972
Vladimir (Christianized Russia, 992),   972-1015
Yaroslaf (The Legislator),   1015-1054
(Close of Heroic Period.)
Isiaslaf,   1054-1078
Vsevolod,   1078-1093
Sviatopolk,   1093-1113
Vladimir Monomakh,   1113-1125
(Throne Disputed by Prince of Suzdal.)
Isiaslaf,   1146-1155
George Dolgoruki (Last Grand Prince of Kief)   1155-1169
(Fall of Kief, 1169.)
Andrew Bogoliubski (First Grand Prince of Suzdal),   1169-1174
George II. (Dolgoruki),   1212-1238
Yaroslaf II. (Father of Alexander Nevski and Grandfather of Daniel, First Prince of Moscow),
        1238-1246
PRINCES OF MOSCOW.
Daniel (Son of Alexander Nevski), 1260-1303
Iri (George) Danielovich,   1303-1325
Ivan I.,   1328-1341
Simeon (The Proud),   1341-1353
Ivan II. (The Debonair),   1353-1359
PRINCES OF MOSCOW AND GRAND PRINCES OF SUZDAL.
Dmitri Donskoi,   1363-1389
Vasili Dmitrievich, 1389-1425
Vasili I. (The Blind, Prince of Moscow, Novgorod, and Suzdal), 1425-1462
GRAND PRINCES OF ALL THE RUSSIAS.
Ivan III. (The Great),   1462-1505
Vasili II.,   1505-1533
TSARS OF RUSSIA.
Ivan IV. (the Terrible),   1533-1584
Feodor Ivanovich,   1584-1598

Boris Godunof (Usurper),   1598-1605
The False Dmitri,   1605-1606
Vasili Shuiski,   1606-1609
Mikhail Romanoff,   1613-1645
Alexis (Son of former and Father of Peter the Great),   1645-1676
Feodor Alexievich,   1676-1682
Ivan V. and Peter I.   )
Sophia Regent,   ) Ivan died 1696   1682-1696
Peter I. (The Great), 1696-1725
Catherine I., 1725-1727
Peter II. (Son of Alexis and Grandson of Peter the Great and Eudoxia),   1727-1730
Anna Ivanovna (Daughter of Ivan V., Niece of Peter I.),   1730-1740
Ivan VI. (Infant Nephew of former Sovereign),   1740-1741
Elizabeth Petrovna (Daughter of Peter I. and Catherine),   1741-1761
Peter III. (Nephew of Elizabeth Petrovna; reigned five months, assassinated),   1762
Catherine II. (Wife of Peter III.),   1762-1796
Paul I. (Son of former),   1796-1801
Alexander I.,1801-1825
Nicholas I., 1825-1855
Alexander II.,   1855-1881
Alexander III.,   1881-1894
Nicholas II., 1894-

15185651R00066

Printed in Great Britain
by Amazon.co.uk, Ltd.,
Marston Gate.